GODDESS POWER

Awakening the Wisdom of the Divine Feminine in Your Life

*For Gindy Ma,
With love, gratitude
and blessings!
Namaste, Isabella*

ISABELLA PRICE

Foreword by Anodea Judith, PhD, author of the
bestselling *Wheels of Life*

For permission requests, please contact the publisher at:

Mango Publishing Group
2850 Douglas Road, 3rd Floor
Coral Gables, FL 33134 USA
info@mango.bz

For special orders, quantity sales, course adoptions and corporate sales, please email the publisher at sales@mango.bz. For trade and wholesale sales, please contact Ingram Publisher Services at customer.service@ingramcontent.com or +1.800.509.4887.

Goddess Power: Awakening the Wisdom of the Divine Feminine in Your Life

Library of Congress Cataloging
ISBN: (print) 978-1-63353-673-9, (ebook) 978-1-63353-674-6
Library of Congress Control Number: 9781633536739
BISAC category code : OCC019000 BODY, MIND & SPIRIT / Inspiration & Personal Growth SEL021000 SELF-HELP / Motivational & Inspirational

Printed in the United States of America

Goddess Power is a fascinating "herstory" of the Divine Feminine, rich in heart, depth and wisdom. Isabella Price's intelligent and well—researched book offers us an empowering message of hope and inspiration that provides a pathway toward a new, more integrated and healthy partnership between the feminine and the masculine. This is a necessary and urgently needed guide to move us toward the next stage of our collective evolution.

— **Katherine Woodward Thomas**, NYT bestselling author of *Calling in "The One"*

Isabella Price's *Goddess Power* is an important book for the emergence of a balanced and embodied consciousness, highlighting the importance of the Divine Feminine. With solid research into history and mythology, this book is an essential bridge that weaves the fabric of reality back into its essential wholeness. True integration combines masculine and feminine in a way that understands the contribution of both. *Goddess Power* embodies that understanding in a style that is fresh, rich, and immediately accessible.

— **Anodea Judith**, PhD, bestselling author of *Wheels of Life*; *The Global Heart Awakens*; *Eastern Body, Western Mind*; *Creating on Purpose*; *Chakra Yoga*

This book speaks to a whole new generation of women who seek to know the energies of the Goddess or Divine Feminine. Isabella Price has done her homework. She knows the power of the Goddess in ancient cultures, and she shares the her—story revealed by modern women of the Goddess movement (Merlin Stone, Marija Gimbutas, Riane Eisler). Bless her for carrying on this sacred lineage of priestesses—ancient and modern—around the world.

—**Vicki Noble**, co—creator of *Motherpeace Tarot*, author of *Shakti Woman* and *The Double Goddess*

Isabella Price distills and synthesizes a vast cross—culture scholarship on the goddesses, making this growing body of scholarly work accessible for a popular audience. She bridges ancient beliefs and practices from the Goddess traditions to postmodern sensibilities, always writing in a respectful voice. Her perspective on Goddess spirituality is guided by the moral fruits that these spiritual teachings inspire, with an eye towards the highest values of the human spirit, including creativity, vitality, nonviolence, collaborative partnership, humane behavior and reverence for the Earth.

— **Karen A. Jaenke**, PhD, Consciousness & Transformative Studies Program Chair John F. Kennedy University

Goddess Power is a substantial, insightful, and accessible book on the wisdom legacy of the Sacred Feminine/ Goddess across cultures. Isabella Price's depth of knowledge, her dedication and passion for the Goddess steeped in her personal experience are felt throughout this treasure of a book. The wisdom of the Sacred Feminine is urgently needed in our times to restore the Earth and uplift humanity. Isabella's *Goddess Power* offers an empowering, joyful, and inspiring vision!

— **Corinne McLaughlin**, co—author, *The Practical Visionary* and *Spiritual Politics*

In *Goddess Power*, Isabella Price gives voice to a lost "herstory." This book is a great read written with such heart and dedication to the path of the Divine Feminine. The Goddess is the essential backbone for the empowered Feminine to rise. For centuries, the wisdom legacy of the Divine Feminine/Goddess has been suppressed, ignored, or distorted. But her archetypal stories hold a golden key of how to stand in a greater truth. Isabella's profound insights and her substantial knowledge about the Goddess traditions help us to re—awaken this power in ourselves.

— **Rev. Christy Michaels**, MA, priestess, ceremonialist, seminary teacher at Gospel of Mary Magdalene

Goddess Power is an important and insightful contribution to scholarship about the Goddess/Divine Feminine and the role of how women have shaped our civilization and history. In her book, Isabella Price traces many paths that open the door for every woman to learn and celebrate her own legacy. Isabella's compassion and wisdom – gleaned from her many years of research and walking the path of the Goddess – surfaces on each page. She is a gifted storyteller. *Goddess Power* is a beautiful book that inspires us to remember and honor the wisdom legacy of the Goddess while also offering a new and empowering vision for our times. It is a book that I will reread and share with my students!

— **Tricia Grame**, PhD, artist, curator, Women's Spirituality adjunct professor at CIIS

In the vast Goddess literature, *Goddess Power* stands out in several ways. With obvious appreciation and reverent delight, Isabella Price introduces us to both the lighter and darker aspects of the Goddess. Informed by her comparative, cross—cultural perspective – including Jungian psychology and integral theory – Isabella helps us relate with both discernment and devotional recognition to numerous archetypes of the Goddess. *Goddess Power* is groundbreaking, highly accessible 21st— century scholarship. I hope it finds many receptive readers!

— **Saniel Bonder**, author of *Healing the Spirit/Matter Split, Waking Down, The White—Hot Yoga of the Heart*

I have read Isabella Price's book *Goddess Power* with much joy. Steeped in the diverse and rich divine feminine traditions for two decades myself, I can confirm her depth of knowledge and her ability to write in an accessible and intelligent way. Each goddess deserves a whole book unto herself but Isabella Price was able to convey the essence of each in this gem of a book. *Goddess Power* reads smoothly, giving you a good taste of her manifestations, leaving you hungry for more. A worthy and beautiful book that I gladly recommend!

— **Nicola Amadora**, PhD, psychologist, spiritual teacher, speaker, women's leadership educator

TABLE OF CONTENTS

FOREWORD

Isabella Price's leading—edge book *Goddess Power* takes us on an inspirational journey into the core of the rich wisdom legacy of the Goddess, worshipped throughout cultures and known by many names, symbol—rich manifestations and archetypal narratives. Isabella is a gifted storyteller who has the ability to write in an accessible and intelligent way. The story of the Goddess is our story, the story of birth, childhood, adulthood, and death, the story of love and healing, and the story of renewal and evolutionary change.

In a world out of balance, teetering on the brink of disaster, we are in desperate need for words of wisdom to guide us. At the root of our problems lies the imbalance between masculine and feminine, apparent not only in the social standing of men and women, but in the archetypal values each domain provides our society. Without addressing the essential missing piece of the Divine Feminine, we cannot reach wholeness, individually or collectively, and cannot come into balance with the Earth. Without the Goddess to give birth to a new world, we have no future.

Goddess Power is a substantial read filled with profound insights on the Divine Feminine/Goddess. Each sentence conveys Isabella's compassion, sensitivity, and the depth gleaned from decades of research, teachings, travels, and participation in numerous rituals and spiritual practices across cultures and religions.

Isabella's book offers an empowering message on how we might evolve toward higher consciousness by reframing unconscious cultural stereotypes and integrating both the healthy "masculine" *and* the healthy "feminine" archetypes to be better prepared for the re—emergence of the Divine Feminine in our times. This integration is essential for both men and women to become *whole* and participate as conscious co—creators in manifesting a new and more holistic vision for our planet.

Anodea Judith

Novato, CA

INTRODUCTION

Loud voices have alleged incompatible differences between
the Abrahamic traditions: Judaism, Christianity, and
Islam. But must there be a clash of civilizations complete
with a never—ending threat of terrorism, destruction,
and violence? Must we continue insisting on differences
of doctrine and ritual that lead to division, intolerance,
discrimination, and conflict? Or can we choose to focus
on beliefs and values held in common, paving the way
for a more inclusive, cooperative, and peaceful world?
I do not suggest that anyone deny or devalue his or
her own religion – quite the contrary. I believe that a
cross—cultural comparative perspective brings a deeper
understanding of one's own favored tradition or practice.
I experienced this phenomenon myself when my study
of Buddhism opened the door for me to an in—depth
understanding of Jesus Christ's original teachings.

The basic belief of religious pluralism is that there is
truth in every spiritual tradition; and a similarly ethical
framework which values compassion, humility, and
charity. The interfaith orientation of this series recognizes
that these ethical values are universal. Adherents of
different religious denominations can coexist in mutual
respect and equal dignity. These are also the ideals
of the Founding Fathers of the United States, and are

represented by organizations such as the Parliament of World Religions. It is in this spirit of unity—within—diversity that I have written *One Truth, Many Paths*.

Integral Theory

I have researched the world's major religions, mythologies, and cultural histories using the new discipline of Integral philosophy. Integral theorists such as Ken Wilber have an all—inclusive view that acknowledges *all* of the wisdom traditions. Integral philosophy also incorporates modern scientific research from psychology, physics, and biology within its theoretical framework. Integral theory then applies contemporary evolutionary theory and the findings of developmental psychology to explain the unfolding of the different stages and structures in the development of human history, culture, and consciousness—including psycho—spiritual development. Integral philosophy offers a helpful perspective when analyzing the different perceptions of Jesus Christ or the evolving notions of the divine. For example, God, or Spirit, can be experienced in three primary and distinct ways:

1. God as Self or the "Great I" (first person or subjective)

2. God as the "Great Thou" or the "Holy Other" (second person or relational)

3. God as the "Great It," the Ground of Being or the Great Web of Life (third person or objective)

According to Wilber, all three ways, or "Faces of God," need to be embraced and integrated to bring about complete spiritual awakening.

Incorporating Myth into Integral Philosophy

Integral philosophy has made great strides in synthesizing modern science, evolutionary perspectives, and philosophical analysis of the world's wisdom traditions – but in his more recent work Ken Wilber ignores the significance of mythic themes and their impact on the modern and postmodern Western world. Integral theory locates mythology at the pre—modern stage of consciousness, where it is perceived as a historical—factual account. However, I believe that the symbolic—metaphoric dimensions of mythology can still offer inspiration to our modern and postmodern world. It is my conviction that mythic narratives are alive or dead, not true or wrong – but they need to be reinterpreted and updated. Myths have been a constant among all cultures throughout time and history. If revitalized, myths can still be relevant today.

Incorporating the Sacred Feminine

Interestingly, I noted that many classics on comparative religion exclude the idea of the Sacred Feminine, perhaps because they were primarily written by men. Books with an emphasis on Goddess symbolism and women's history have been written over the last few decades, usually from a predominantly feminist perspective; but, strangely, studies on comparative religion generally reduce mention of the Sacred Feminine to a few sentences. It is time to change this. To dismiss or denigrate an expression of the divine that can be traced back to the Paleolithic and Neolithic eras, and which continues to play an important role in practices such as the vibrant *Shakta*—tradition of India, is to tell only half of the story of our human experience.

In India, the Divine Mother represents the activating principle in the manifest world of matter. She is the indwelling divine, present in all being. In Jewish mysticism, the Holy Feminine—referred to as *Shekinah*— fulfills a similar function. Taoism's most famous symbols, the "yin" (feminine principle) and "yang" (masculine principle), are in constant interplay. Yin and yang are not considered rigid, incompatible polarities—rather they complement each other; together they form the universe. Historically, a rigid and exclusive gender hierarchy has been particularly apparent in the emergence of patriarchal structures and paradigms across cultures and religious traditions. As a result, a "harmonious balance" has been sacrificed. Today, more than ever, we need to regain balance for the sake of our survival as human species, and to restore the ecological balance of our planet and its equally precious other—than—human life forms.

The Three Pillars of *One Truth, Many Paths*

What is praised is one, so the praise is one too,

many jugs being poured into a huge basin.

All religions, all the singing, one song.

The differences are just illusion and vanity.

Sunlight looks slightly different

on this wall than it does on that wall

and a lot different on this other one, but

it is still one light . . .

—Rumi

Saints and mystics across cultures and religions talk of a universal and inclusive God of love, compassion, and forgiveness. They view love as the basis of all reality and the force that drives evolution. Many mystics and saints have suggested that all life is sacred. They see us as one human family. They emphasize the interdependence and interrelatedness of all phenomena in the great cosmic web of Being. Indeed, representatives of all the major wisdom traditions have all taught the Golden Rule: "Do unto others as you would have them do unto you." The universality of ethical precepts—compassion being a core value—is just one aspect of our common spiritual heritage.

The *One Truth, Many Paths Series* focuses on three guiding principles found in every religious tradition, and which I call pillars:

1. Shared ethical systems and precepts

2. The esoteric—mystical core of each wisdom tradition

3. Universal symbols and archetypes present in religious myths of all traditions

Pillar One – Ethical Systems and Precepts

Ethical injunctions are an integral part of the scriptures and moral codes in all the wisdom traditions. For example, selfless service to the community is always considered an act of love and generosity that confers spiritual benefits. Ethical systems and precepts may have originated as a way of preventing social chaos and anarchy.

Pillar Two – The Esoteric—Mystical Core

The esoteric—mystical core in each wisdom tradition is another unifying principle. This core is sometimes referred to as "inner faith," an awareness of the divine within one's own being. Indeed, mystics of different faiths may feel more affinity for one another than they do for members of their own religions who emphasize only "external" aspects such as the proper way to conduct rituals, the adherence to particular dress codes, or the insistence on an exclusively literal—factual interpretation of scripture.

Pillar Three – Universal Symbols and Archetypes

The third pillar of commonality is that similar universal archetypes can be found in every religion. In this series, I focus on the following three major archetypes: The Mother, the Father, and the Savior—Hero. The idea of an archetype comes from the work of Swiss psychologist Carl Gustav Jung, who suggested that several basic archetypes or "patterns" can be found in our shared human "collective unconscious." Archetypes have shaped religious myths across cultures.

The Mother Archetype was celebrated in numerous ancient religious rituals as a sacred marriage between a goddess and a king. The worship of the archetypal "Great Mother" can be traced to the Paleolithic period more than 20,000 years ago. The Mother archetype represents the nurturing, healing, and life—giving powers; but can alternatively take on fiercer, destructive, terrifying forms—especially when associated with the phenomenon of death and dissolution. Examples of the Mother archetype include the Christian conception of Mother Mary, the *Shakta* conception of the goddess Kali in India, and the New Age conception of the Earth as Gaia.

The Father Archetype has been honored in many patriarchal societies and cultures ranging from the Abrahamic traditions to the mythology of classical Greece, where Zeus, the thunderbolt—brandishing "Sky God," was worshipped as "Father—Chief" of the Olympian pantheon of deities. As with the Mother archetype, the concept of God as a Father takes two modes. God can be viewed as all—merciful, compassionate, forgiving, and caring – a father who watches over "his" creation from "above." Or God can alternatively be seen as stern, angry, merciless, and punitive – a judge who rewards the "righteous" and punishes "evildoers." The idea of a vengeful Father—God has been used to justify acts of violence committed in "his" name against "unbelievers."

The Savior—Hero Archetype is encountered in all the wisdom traditions, and has inspired a rich legacy of mythic narratives recounting many great and wondrous deeds spanning the savior's early childhood to death – as, for example, in the well—documented life of Lord Krishna in India. In his classical study *The Hero with a Thousand Faces*, mythologist Joseph Campbell identified a universal pattern or structure that marks the journey of all savior—heroes: birth into the ordinary world; the call to adventure; a refusal of the call; meeting with a mentor and other helpers and allies; crossing the first threshold (tests, trials, and ordeals); a reward; resurrection; and the return to the community with the elixir of life. Savior—heroes earn lasting fame by performing great deeds and by instructing the members of their society in appropriate values and behavior patterns. Savior—heroes are willing to pay the ultimate price by sacrificing their own life on behalf of an ideal or a community.

Shared universal symbols are found as well, in particular that of the World Tree, Cosmic Tree, Tree of Life, also known as the *axis mundi* or world axis. These symbols and archetypes provide inspiration and facilitate our psycho—

spiritual empowerment in this complex and ever—
evolving, ever—unfolding universe.

Additional Dimensions

I emphasize our shared symbolic—mythological
heritage and the universality of ethical—moral tenets,
but acknowledge that religions are *not* all the same. I
see them as equally valuable but different, and do not
take a position on the legitimacy or veracity of *claims of
superiority* or *uniqueness* in regard to religious figures,
doctrine, and belief systems. In order to best understand
each individual religion, we need to know the historical—
cultural context in which it developed. We need to take
external factors into consideration. These are factors that
vary greatly from culture to culture. The same factors are
subject to change as societies and cultures evolve.

I examine each religious tradition with respect. There is
truth in every religion. It is my conviction that all religious
paths can lead to salvation or liberation if the seeker
has a profound, consistent practice. Spirituality, and the
awareness of our own conscious Being, are integral to the
human experience. The same fundamental questions are
addressed by religious myths in every culture:

- Who are we?
- Where do we come from?
- How do we relate to this universe?
- Where do we go after we die?

One Truth, Many Paths

The approach of this series is to *simplify without
oversimplification*. The material is organized so that

complex subjects can become more easily accessible. Humans have come up with over four thousand different religions. This series aims to provide a concise, balanced, and in—depth introduction to the essence and fundamentals of the five major world religions: Hinduism, Buddhism, Judaism, Christianity, and Islam. Judaism, which has the fewest number of adherents of the five, is nevertheless essential because it is the foundational religion of the two other Abrahamic traditions: Christianity and Islam. Aspects of other wisdom traditions—such as Taoism, Confucianism, Shinto, Zoroastrianism, Jainism, Sikhism, and Baha'i—are interspersed, but included primarily within the context of and in comparison with the five major traditions. Also included (esp. in the upcoming publication, *In the Beginning: Creation Myths Across Cultures*) are discussions of *primal* or *tribal* traditions. Our destruction of the earth's ecological balance shows we must pay more attention to what the primal traditions have to teach us, not less.

Each *One Truth, Many Paths* publication provides an in—depth discussion of an aspect of human spirituality. Each subject area in this tapestry of the human quest to understand Spirit is discussed clearly, and with many examples, to ensure an accurate understanding. The scope of this series is ambitious, ranging from a discussion of ancient pre—modern beliefs to speculations on various New Thought movements and views of the Apocalypse and the Afterlife. I believe our human spirituality will evolve as we grow as individuals and collectively as a species, and I wish to be of service in this endeavor.

An Overview of My Journey

My research took me to sacred sites in India, Egypt, Israel, Turkey, Italy, Greece, Indonesia, Vietnam,

Cambodia, Japan, the United States and other nations. I have put years into the study of spiritual and religious texts. My journey began with my horror over the events of 9/11, and finished with reverence for the human reaching for the divine – which takes many paths worldwide, but which, in essence, always seems to arrive at the same one simple truth. My goal has been to contribute to a deeper understanding between cultures and religions, in hope of a lasting global peace.

My professional experience includes the teaching of World History and Religion courses in academic institutions in Switzerland and California. I have studied Buddhism at the Buddha Gate Monastery in California, and repeatedly visited the ashram of Sri Mata Amritanandamayi Devi (known to millions of people worldwide as Amma, which means spiritual Mother, Mother of Compassion, Mother of Immortal Bliss). Amma is also called "The Hugging Saint." Her religion is "love."

I have participated in religious rituals across the spectrum of wisdom traditions, ranging from numerous Native American rituals in the Lakota tradition to Jewish Holy Day gatherings with Rabbi Michael Lerner's *Tikkun* community, which showed me that Judaism's love and generosity reaches across class, gender, racial, and religious divides. I have also participated in prayer practices with members of the Muslim community. All of these experiences across the spiritual traditions have been deeply emotionally moving to me. There are many of us, worldwide, who share the belief that there is an *equal amount of truth in all wisdom traditions*, and I hope to see this mutual respect and understanding grow. Thank you for being a part of this intellectual, metaphysical and spiritual journey.

"I who am the beauty of the green earth and the white moon among the stars

and the mysteries of the waters, I call upon your soul to arise and come unto me.

For I am the soul of nature that gives life to the universe. From me all things proceed

and unto me they must return. Let my worship be in the heart that rejoices, for behold –

all acts of love and pleasure are my rituals. Let there be beauty and strength, power

and compassion, honor and humility, mirth and reverence within you. And you who

seek to know me, know that...if that which you seek, you find not within yourself,

you will never find it without. For behold, I have been with you from the beginning,

and I am that which is attained at the end of desire"[1]
(The Charge of the Goddess)

---

[1] Quoted from Starhawk, *Spiral Dance*, p.102—03.

AN OVERVIEW OF GODDESS WORSHIP

In 1976, art historian Merlin Stone wrote that at the dawn of religion God was a woman. She is referring to the Paleolithic period, more than twenty thousand years ago, when *homo sapiens sapiens* first responded with spiritual awe to the swelling of women's bellies and the miracle of life that came forth from their wombs. As our ancestors struggled to survive, they created carvings of the pregnant Mother as a sacred symbol imbued with life force. The Mother Goddess was viewed as the Divine Feminine, the great matrix of creation, with life—giving and sustaining powers. As the *Charge of the Goddess* so beautifully expresses, the Goddess is earth, the nurturing mother who brings forth the manifest world. She is the power of fertility, the womb of creation and creativity. As earth, the Goddess embodies all life; she is immanent or indwelling in all of creation. She is the tree, leaf, plant, wind, river, lake, bud, flower, fur, claw, and fang. She is the pregnant Paleolithic Mother, the Neolithic bird and snake goddess, or the "Lady of the Beasts" flanked by lions. The Goddess is present in the form of energy, even in seemingly inanimate objects such as rocks and stones. She governs the elemental forces of nature. Yet, she is also the celestial Goddess, the morning and evening star, or the moon that symbolizes women's menstrual cycles. The moon rules the tides of the oceans – the watery womb of the first microorganisms – and the waves of the lakes and rivers that are the arteries of Mother Earth. Moreover, the moon is symbolically associated with profound feelings and emotions that wash over us like waves.

As the moon, the Goddess has three aspects: As she waxes, she is the maiden or virgin; full, she is the mother; and as she wanes, she is the crone or wise woman. As the feminine triad of virgin, mother, and crone, infusing the manifest world with change and transformation, the Goddess is the living body of a sacred organic universe. She is life eternally attempting to reproduce, regenerate, and sustain itself – and she represents a force that is even more implacable than death, although death is ultimately an aspect of life as well.

As an expression of the mystery of the ever—unfolding life cycle, the Goddess also serves as a model for re—sacralizing woman's body and sexuality. As humans, we literally carry the biochemical components of Gaia, also known as Mother Earth, in our physical bodies. Goddess religion trusts the wisdom that comes through our bodies, and identifies sexuality as the expression of the creative life force of the universe. Sexuality is considered sacred because it is a sharing of energy that occurs while in passionate surrender to the power of the Goddess. As the *Charge of the Goddess* puts it, "All acts of love and pleasure are my rituals." In Goddess religion, *flesh and spirit* are *one*.

According to Starhawk, author, feminist, and cofounder of the Wiccan Reclaiming Collective, the symbolism of the Goddess is not a parallel structure to the archetype of "God the Father." The Goddess does not rule the world nor is she separate from it. She *is* the world, manifest in each being. The Goddess does *not* exclude the male: she contains him, as a pregnant woman contains a male child. Although the divine is ultimately seen as one, pagan rituals conceptualize the divine as having both female *and* male aspects. Two of the oldest forms of the divine – the great Goddess and her consort, the Horned God – illustrate this concept. The conception of a single divine force containing both male and female aspects can be found in the mythologies of many cultures. One of its most enduring expressions – still celebrated today with variations in numerous religious traditions – is the ritualistic sacred marriage originating from ancient Mesopotamia.

The Divine Feminine also represents death and dissolution. Just as everything originates from the Mother Goddess...in the end, everything returns. Birth, growth, decay, and death are sacred stages within the life cycle. The Goddess also governs the destructive elemental forces of nature manifesting as volcanic eruptions and devastating floods. In her fierce and terrifying manifestations, the Goddess is the Dark Mother who dances on cremation grounds and appears at crossroads and pivotal junctures in our lives. She demands that we face our repressed "shadow" issues and embark on our arduous night journey of the soul, going beyond our attachments and limitations. The Dark Mother embodies the great dissolution: ego—death and physical death. She symbolizes the pearls of wisdom to be gleaned from the "Great Below." At the esoteric—mystical level, the Goddess invites us to delve into the mystery of Being, and Goddess worship helps us rediscover the infinite freedom of Being within our true Self. She is a bridge to this Self, which is the source of our innate talents and creativity, and encourages us to overcome limiting cultural and personal conditioning so we can manifest our fullest potential. To "know oneself" has since ancient times been the core principle within all pagan mystery religions. Aspirants were initiated into the essence of being which allowed them to see the true nature of reality. The Goddess is the ship on which we may sail the deep uncharted seas within. She is the gate through which we may pass into the eternal now.

At the exoteric—external level, the *Charge of the Goddess* – a core liturgy text – is read by pagan communities and Wiccan covens throughout the world. The term *wicca* derives from an Anglo—Saxon root word meaning to "bend or shape" and refers to the wise women – notably healers, teachers, poets, and midwives – who seek to shape the unseen to their will. Goddess—centered religions such as Wicca are a viable spiritual path that began at the dawn of human civilization. Today, these religions offer a potent constellation of psycho—spiritual, ecological, and political ideas focusing on the conception of femininity as divine. Many people consider a belief in the Divine Feminine to be an essential counter—balance to our overly masculinized contemporary culture.

After millennia of suppression of the Divine Feminine, as a result of the increasingly patriarchal paradigms that emerged in all systems of organized religion across the cultural spectrum, the Goddess is once again becoming a powerful symbol for what is most needed in our modern and postmodern times. Paganism and Wiccan rituals throughout the world honor and celebrate the Goddess as a catalyst for an emerging spirituality that is earth—centered and cares for the earth as a living organism, protects natural resources for future generations, and hopes to keep our populations in balance with the natural environment in the understanding that all of life is interrelated and inherently sacred. What affects one part, ultimately affects the whole in this great cosmic web. Such an understanding generally fosters more compassion and a stronger desire for social justice. The Goddess reminds us that our spirituality does not take us *out* of the world, but rather brings us more fully *in*.

GODDESS BELIEF SYSTEMS AND THE BODY—MIND SPLIT

The Goddess invites us to engage in this world by taking action to preserve all life on earth, to help alleviate poverty, to speak the truth about pain and suffering, and to resolve conflicts peacefully. Being on the path of the Goddess is consistent with a commitment to acting with integrity and generosity, to taking responsibility for the community of Being outside ourselves, and to becoming more attuned to our own embodied awareness. The primary focus of Goddess religion is on transforming through intimate interactions and common struggles to build harmonious multicultural societies among different ethnic groups. The same principles apply to gender relations. Goddess spirituality does not legitimize the rule of either sex by the other. In her groundbreaking study *The Chalice and the Blade*, Riane Eisler talks about the "partnership model," in which social relations are based on the principle of "linking" rather than "ranking" during the period of prehistory, that is, before the invention of the writing systems roughly by the end of the fourth millennium BCE. According to Eisler, cultural transformation theory suggests that the original direction of our cultural evolution was geared toward partnership but that, following a period of chaos and almost total cultural disruption, a fundamental social shift occurred. The title of Eisler's book derives from this dramatic turning point at the dawn of civilization when the cultural evolution of societies that worshiped the life—generating and nurturing powers of the universe – symbolized by the

ancient chalice or grail – was interrupted by Indo—
European invaders who worshiped the power of the
blade, that is, the power to take rather than to give
life. According to Eisler, it was the power of the blade
that ultimately led to the establishment of patriarchal
domination systems. Similarly, in her more recent book
Urgent Message from Mother, feminist activist Jean Shinoda
Bolen argues that the "feminine" – the Divine Mother –
does indeed represent life while the "masculine" principle
increasingly stands for death, as exemplified by the
frightening accumulation of weapons of mass destruction
over the last few decades.

The path of the Goddess stands in sharp contrast to the
patriarchal conditioning that occurred over the centuries
in basically all of the world's major religious systems.
This conditioning led to a profound body—mind—split
insofar as it repeatedly emphasized the necessity of
transcending the manifest world of form considered
inferior to Spirit. That is, the patriarchal religious
traditions focused their teachings and practices on the
transcendence of the human body, sexuality, and all the
affairs of the so—called "mundane" world. With
few exceptions, such as, for example, the tantric
traditions, and ever since the great religious systems
emerged during the period of what integral theory calls
traditional—mythic consciousness, Spirit has been
regarded as being incompatible with what we may call
"embodied consciousness" or innate "body wisdom." And
this is still a widely held belief today. This body—mind—
split is the great paradox, the unresolved wound that lies
at the core of the human condition and has been carried
into our modern and postmodern times, as integral
spiritual teachers and founders of the *Waking Down in
Mutuality* approach, Saniel and Linda Bonder,
have repeatedly emphasized.

CONTROVERSIES ON THE EVOLUTION OF GODDESS WORSHIP

Marija Gimbutas, pioneering archaeologist and cultural historian of Neolithic "Old Europe," has, since the 1970's, been a major authority for the Goddess quest. Gimbutas recounts a time before patriarchy, warfare, domination, and social stratification when humans lived together peacefully and were in harmony with nature. According to her, this was a period in which both men and women revered the feminine principle as the immanent power of renewal that carried life through creation, growth, decay, death, and, eventually, rebirth. Goddess—worshipping societies enjoyed material abundance and an equitable distribution of wealth. These societies existed without oppressive hierarchies of any kind, according to Gimbutas. She suggests that these egalitarian, peaceful communities emerged during the Paleolithic period and lasted well into the agricultural transition of the Neolithic; and she argues that cultures that worshipped the Goddess were not restricted to areas of the Balkans and the northeastern Mediterranean, but could be found worldwide.

In her work, Gimbutas places a great emphasis on the predominance of female figurines. She identifies these prehistoric objects as expressions of a "unitary Goddess" who governed the cycle of birth, death, and regeneration. The most basic argument for the theory of a "unitary Goddess" may be found in the fundamental questions that likely arose during the prehistoric period: "Where were we humans before we were born?" and "Where do we go after we die?" Obviously, our human ancestors observed that new life emerges from the body of woman. The basic biological fact that the life—giving powers rest in the female must have left them in a state of awe and wonderment at the great miracle of birth. It appears thus quite plausible that the earliest representations of supernatural powers should have taken a female rather than a male form. Certainly, it would have been natural for our ancestors to imagine the universe as an all—giving, all—caring Mother from whose womb life emerges, and back to which life eventually returns, like the process of rebirth in vegetative cycles. Thus it makes sense that women were respected, rather than perceived as subservient. These cultures conceptualized the powers governing the universe in female form, which led to qualities such as caring, compassion, and nonviolence being highly valued. That does not imply that these were matriarchal societies, that is, societies in which women dominated men. Rather, it appears likely that the sexes were perceived as complementing each other.

It should be noted that some feminist archaeologists and scholars have rejected the notion of a unitary "Great Goddess," and have been critical of Gimbutas' assertion that the prehistoric culture was "female—dominated." Their primary argument lies in the difficulty of any attempt to reconstruct prehistoric religious beliefs. This is mostly due to the lack of written records, a fact that leaves archaeological evidence open to a wide range of interpretation. Written sources are important to understanding the religion of a culture: they provide a context and an explanation for the use of any excavated objects. Feminist scholars such as Rosemary Radford Ruether have stressed that the predominance of female religious imagery does not necessarily mean that women enjoyed a higher status, as we see in contemporary India or during the medieval period in Europe. Finally, the validity of a theory asserting that successive incursions of Indo—European invaders were the sole cause for the transformation of Southern—European and Mediterranean cultures from a peaceful matrifocal orientation to a patriarchal and militaristic one, has also been questioned by non—feminist scholars and archaeologists. The path that led from the early Neolithic towns – in which agriculture, domesticated animals, textiles, pottery, and trade flourished – to the hierarchical, slave—owning cities of the Sumerian world with their royal and priestly classes, temples, palaces, and organized warfare a few millennia later, is not necessarily a straight evolutionary line but was likely a much more complex and multi—faceted process.

The major stimulus for this evolutionary process came – according to Radford Ruether and other feminist scholars – less from outside nomadic invaders on horseback, and more from gradual internal developments that were triggered by the accumulation of wealth in the hands of an elite. Another interesting approach comes from Leonard Shlain, author of *The Alphabet versus the Goddess: The Conflict between Word and Image*. Shlain proposes that the invention of script at around 3000 BCE, and the process of acquiring the skills of alphabetic literacy, reinforced the brain's linear, abstract, and predominantly "masculine" left hemisphere at the expense of the holistic, iconic, and "feminine" right one. This shift upset the balance between men and women, initiating the disappearance of Goddess worship, the abhorrence of images, and, finally, the decline of women's political status in the early stages of alphabetic literacy.

While this major historical controversy may never be fully resolved, it is nevertheless understandable that the idea of a primeval, peaceful, and matrifocal world in Europe and the Mediterranean area during Paleolithic and Neolithic times became popular in our postmodern time. Many people are drawn by the allure of a peaceful, egalitarian, and ecologically sustainable future. Clearly, this is an enormously appealing vision, particularly for women. By imagining an idyllic past, the exploitation of nature and patriarchal domination lose their claim to primacy. Further, the assertion that these patriarchal paradigms represent a so—called "natural order" is challenged. In fact, from the perspective of the proponents of a unitary "Great Goddess" theory, patriarchal domination just becomes a bad interlude that can, and should, be transcended in order to restore wholesome balance to our planet. Values such as equality, community, partnership, cooperation, and non—violence reflect what author and psychotherapist Anodea Judith, author of *Waking the Global Heart,* calls the archetypal "Dynamic Feminine."

GODDESS WORSHIP AND INTEGRAL THEORY

When viewed from the framework of integral theory –
based on philosopher Ken Wilber's pioneering work
– and its different stages of consciousness and culture,
"feminine" values represent world—centric paradigms
that are characteristic of the postmodernist stage,
or the "green values—system" according to the theory
of human development known as Spiral Dynamics.
The "Dynamic Feminine" is highly resistant to both
conformist authoritarian structures (blue values—system)
and capitalistic acquisition and exploitation of nature
and people (orange values—system). The green values—
system is *not* yet integral, but this cultural stage
constitutes an evolutionary step on the trajectory toward
the integral stage of consciousness and beyond. In this
evolutionary context, it may be helpful to consider an
additional viewpoint.

Elizabeth Debold, pioneer in women's development,
feminist thinker, and senior editor of what was known as
EnlightenNext magazine (previously *What is Enlightenment?*
Issue March—May 2006), suggests that we may attempt
to reach *beyond* the different notions of feminine
and masculine altogether. Even though Debold fully
acknowledges the importance for modern and postmodern
Western culture to radically reconnect with the sacredness
of life – a notion that is an intrinsic part of the Divine
Feminine – she also argues that notions such as these,
if tied *exclusively* to the feminine, evoke the personal and
cultural past of women with its legacy of suffering and
victimization that has so deeply shaped our selves and

society. Ideas of gender as expressed and defined by the Divine Feminine, or whatever we may associate with it on an individual and collective level, harbor, according to Debold, the potential of preventing us from transcending the very gender polarities we ultimately strive to free ourselves from. In other terms, visions related to a more life—enhancing future that are bound up in our ideas of being women or men, may prove counter—productive in the end because they hold us back from transcending our gender's grip on our consciousness.

Debold goes on to point out that images of goddesses and gods emerged in a pre—literate time, when the human capacity to conceptualize and think in terms of higher abstraction was limited. Premodern visions, as expressed in the forms of female and male deities, tie us to a "primitive duality." Debold argues that the breaking of this pattern – which is also bound together in a hierarchy of domination and subordination – cannot come about by making the feminine superior. Debold concludes that claims to the superiority of the Divine Feminine only perpetuate a pattern, instead of serving as a cure for the abuses of power that are destroying our world.

Similarly, a recent comprehensive study, *The Evolutionary Journey of Woman: From the Goddess to Integral Feminism* by scholar and author Sarah Nicholson, explores women's developmental journey in Western culture from the perspective of integral theory, feminist theory, and transpersonal psychology. In addition to tracing women's rich contributions to the evolution of culture, alongside the painful history of their oppression, Nicholson envisions a future that integrates women's past wisdom with present and future potentialities of self—realization.

We may also note in this context that integral theory views patriarchy generally as an unavoidable "arrangement" between the sexes that was an important part of human development at earlier stages but does no longer serve its evolutionary purpose and hence needs to be "deconstructed" and transcended. I argue that the postmodernist stage with its reemphasis on the Goddess and "feminine" paradigms and values systems commonly associated with it (most prominently a caring and earth—centered spirituality), constitutes an indispensable evolutionary milestone on the trajectory toward the integral stage of consciousness and culture. Even so, the notion that the divine can take a female form has yet to enter the consciousness of many people. Honoring the feminine aspects of sacred love does not require that new structures of female domination and superiority have to be established. Respecting the feminine aspects of the divine simply promotes a worldview that is more balanced and complementary. It is my hope that this exploration of the faces, functions, and symbols of the Divine Feminine across our world's many cultures may serve as a gateway and catalyst to conscious evolution. For the first time in recorded history, both men and women have the potential to be true partners and social equals. A truly integral approach allows for both transcendence and inclusion.

GODDESS WORSHIP AND SPIRITUAL VISIONARIES

An answer to the seemingly intractable problem of gender – and the millennia—old legacy of pain and oppression that has come with it – may be found in the thinking of some of the world's spiritual visionaries. Twenty—five hundred years ago the Buddha emphasized that truth and liberation lie beyond all polarities and gender categories. And in the noncanonical Gospel of Thomas, Jesus Christ is reported to have made the following announcement: "When the male will not be male nor the female be female...then you will enter the Kingdom of Heaven" (22:5—7). Finally, renowned Indian mystic Ammachi – also known as the Hugging Saint and Mother of Compassion – comments on the issue of God and gender as follows: "Is God a Man or a Woman? The answer is: *Neither – God is That.* But if you must give God a gender, God is more female than male, for *he* is contained in *She.*" [2]

Ultimately, Spirit is transpersonal in its essence, and any attempt to link the divine *exclusively* to one particular gender or a single anthropomorphic form amounts to a questionable reductionism.

---

[2] Quoted from Canan, *Messages from Amma*, p. 169.

WHAT IS THE DIVINE FEMININE?

The essence of the Divine Feminine is found during the Paleolithic era in representations of the so—called "Great Mother," followed by representative examples of Neolithic bird and snake goddesses. In ancient Mesopotamia ritualistic sacred marriage became an integral part of the emerging religious traditions. The narrative of the Sumerian goddess Inanna's descent to the underworld represents an archetypal journey for spiritual growth. Later, the archetypal mother goddess of ancient Egypt, Isis, was worshiped as a gifted healer, and was also the bringer of civilization and "savior of the human race." The narrative of Isis and Osiris, her consort—brother, with its rich symbolism and resurrection theme, has left a profound mark on Christianity.

Other important manifestations of the Divine Feminine can be found in the premodern civilization of Minoan Crete. Feminist scholars commonly perceive Minoan civilization as the epitome of Goddess culture. Some elements of the sacred rituals of Minoan Crete are said to have survived well into the times of the much more patriarchal culture of classical Greece many centuries later, most prominently exemplified by a ritual known as the Eleusinian Mysteries. On the continent of Africa, the enchanting and seductive goddess Oshun was worshiped by the ancestors of the Yoruba people of present—day Nigeria. Born at the source of the river in Nigeria that bears her name, Oshun was said to bring life and healing wisdom. As a result of the enslavement of thousands of Yoruba men and women who were kidnapped and taken across the Atlantic to the "New World" in the late eighteenth and early nineteenth centuries, Oshun is currently one of the most popular deities in Brazil and in communities of immigrants in Cuba, New York and Miami.

The Virgin Mary, who has the official title of "Queen of Heaven" in the Roman Catholic tradition, is another example of the rich symbolism and importance of the Divine Feminine. The Virgin Mary, who has been set apart from "ordinary" women by the notions of Immaculate Conception and Perpetual Virginity, may be an embodiment of pre—Christian goddesses with their ancient narratives, iconographies, and symbols. Another aspect of the Divine Feminine aspect of sacred love is portrayed by Mother Mary's multiple functions, with her healing capabilities and her intercession on behalf of the souls of the deceased. The Black Madonna is one of her most intriguing manifestations.

Mary Magdalene is another aspect of the Divine Feminine, and a figure who has been the subject of countless controversy and debate among biblical scholars. As the first witness to the resurrection, Mary Magdalene was considered by the apostle John to be the founder of Christianity, though in most theological studies she has, until fairly recently, been depicted as a "reformed prostitute" or "redeemed sinner" who exemplifies Christ's mercy. Mary Magdalene has alternatively been portrayed as the "forgotten bride" of Christianity and even as being married to Jesus Christ – a concept popularized by best—selling books such as Dan Brown's *Da Vinci Code.* Over the last decades, serious research has been conducted to clarify some aspects of her role and function in early Christianity by including both the canonical Gospels and new and interesting perspectives based on information revealed by the noncanonical scriptures.

The rich symbolism and multi—faceted manifestations of the Sacred Feminine takes the form of the goddess Kuan Shi Yin in the Chinese tradition, and Devi in India. A popular manifestation of Devi is Kali, the "Dark Mother." In India, Kali is worshiped as both the benevolent *and* the terrifying Mother who destroys the finite to reveal the Infinite. (Further illumination regarding other Hindu goddesses and Buddhist representations of the Sacred Feminine can be found in the ONE TRUTH, MANY PATHS e—books on Hinduism and Buddhism, respectively. Similarly, the feminine "Face of God" in the Jewish and Islamic traditions will be explored in the e—books on Judaism and Islam, respectively).

The Divine Feminine at its source is one. Yet the Goddess is known by innumerable names and manifestations across the world's cultures. Many of these conceptions are mysterious and seemingly paradoxical. She has been honored and worshiped as the Virgin Mary, Diana, Cerridwen, Hecate, Pele, Inanna, Athena, Demeter, Sarasvati, Kuan Yin, Brigid, Yemaya, Tara, Kali, Asherah, Isis and White Buffalo Calf Woman, to mention just a few. But beneath these many different faces, aspects, and symbols we find the enduring essence of the Divine Feminine...which is always the same.

The Laussel Venus — Gravettian Culture
(Dordogne, France)

PREHISTORIC MANIFESTATIONS OF THE "GREAT GODDESS"

The Paleolithic Mother Goddess

Approximately 20,000 years ago the figure of a woman seventeen inches tall was carved on a limestone slab at the entrance to a rock shelter in Laussel, in the Dordogne, France. In her raised right hand, she holds a bison's horn, crescent—shaped like the moon. Thirteen lines etched on the crescent—horn may refer to the thirteen days of the waxing moon and the thirteen months of the lunar year. With her left hand, the figure points to her swelling womb. An intrinsic connection may exist between the waxing moon and the fecundity of a woman's womb. Traces of red ochre – a surrogate of the life—giving blood of woman – are still visible on this figurine also known as the "Goddess of Laussel." The term commonly used for menstruating women's being on their "moon cycle" may well connect to this sort of ancient symbolic reference. This bountiful Goddess has large, pendulous breasts and broad hips. She is one of many female figurines sculpted on ledges and terraces of rock above the caves where our Paleolithic ancestors lived. The mouth of the cave – that may be interpreted as an analogy to the opening of the female womb – must have been especially sacred. The Laussel shelter itself, with carvings of several other female figurines and representations of animals on the walls, was likely used mainly for ritual and worship.

Many of the naked female figurines that date back to the Paleolithic period appear to be related to pregnancy and the process of giving birth. Their buttocks and thighs are often disproportionately emphasized. Marija Gimbutas interprets this over—emphasis on the generative organs – breasts, vulvas, and buttocks – as a means to magically enhance the sacred life—giving powers of the female body. Yet modern Western culture tends to categorize breasts, vulvas, and buttocks as sex symbols. This may explain why Paleolithic figurines are often called "Venus" figurines by male scholars – an interpretation which reduces the Paleolithic "Mother Goddess" to an "object" intended to arouse sexual desire and doesn't take her rich symbolism into account.

Her vulva – represented by a triangle, oval, open circle, or even by a bud carved on rock walls – symbolized more than human reproduction; it also symbolized the all—encompassing life force that emanates from our earth. The vulva adorned with plants or as a flower bud may have represented the sacred threshold through which all new life emerges. In the *Shakta* tradition of India, the sacred downward pointing triangle still represents the life force of the Divine Mother. The same symbolism can be found in sacred ritualistic diagrams such as, for example, on the Kali *yantra*, which invokes the Goddess.

An equally misguiding characterization of these Paleolithic figurines is the term "fertility idol," because it trivializes their sacred meaning, according to Gimbutas. Fertility is often viewed as an expression of a "primitive" cult that is "inferior" to subsequent "higher" patriarchal systems of institutionalized religion. Yet, how can we know for sure that these figurines are, indeed, goddesses...and not simply the beauties of a local Paleolithic tribe? In the *Myth of the Goddess: Evolution of an Image*, Anne Baring and Jules Cashford argue that the bodies of these female figurines are not naturalistic representations but rather ritualized bodies. Because these figurines represent the drama of birth, they tell us the story of how life comes into being. They are a reflection of the mystery of the unmanifest becoming manifest in the whole of nature. To put it into Baring and Cashford's words, this mystery "far transcends the female body and woman as carrier of this image, for the body of the female of any species leads through the mystery of birth to the mystery of life itself."[3]

Paleolithic cave sanctuaries, figurines, and rites seem to express the belief that human, plant, and animal life all spring from the same source: the "Great Mother," primeval Giver of All, who is known by many different names across the world's cultures. At a time when the survival of humankind was constantly threatened, skilled prehistoric artists must have felt awe at the miracle of birth that was manifested in women's bodies. Further, the archaic—magical worldview of our ancestors recognized

---

[3] Baring and Cashford, *The Myth of the Goddess*, p. 8.

that human beings and all other life forms share an inextricable connection, partaking equally in the cycle of life and death. Consequently, all life forms and nature itself had to be treated with respect.

The same worldview continues into the Neolithic period and beyond. Thousands of figurines and representations of the Sacred Feminine were an integral part of the great river valley civilizations that emerged in the late fourth millennium BCE. In some of these representations, the Goddess is surrounded by symbols of nature such as animals, trees, fruits, water, and stars. During the Neolithic period, the "Great Mother" is sometimes depicted as partly animal and partly human, especially in the cultures of the Near East.

The Neolithic Lady Bird Goddess

Roughly around 10,000 BCE, humans started to transition from active hunter—gatherers to a more sedentary lifestyle based on agriculture and the domestication of animals. This fundamental transition – revolutionary in its scope and long—term impact – led to innovations that affected all aspects of life. A broad and rich array of artifacts from the Neolithic period has been excavated so far. The Neolithic Goddess often appears part woman, part animal. Most of these representations date back to the fourth, fifth, and

Lady Bird, 4th
Millennium BCE

sixth millennia BCE. While the Sacred Feminine has been symbolically related to numerous animals – bird, snake, fish, frog, doe, bear, bee, butterfly, and lionnes to name a few – we will discuss two of her most prominent representations: the Bird Goddess and the Snake Goddess. Additional animal symbols will be examined more extensively in conjunction with goddess figurines from the great civilizations that emerged roughly around 3000 BCE.

During the Neolithic period, the Divine Feminine was sometimes represented as the creative source of all life in the form of a Bird Goddess pregnant with a large egg. This is likely a reference to the mythic cosmic egg that contains the seeds of a new creation. Floating on the primeval waters, the cosmic egg is one of the oldest symbols of life that is found as a theme in basically all of the world's creation myths. The egg is split, and from the two halves the entire world emerges: heaven and earth, female and male. The large egg may have symbolized the primal womb, the matrix of all being. The Neolithic Bird Goddess assumes the nurturing and protective functions of motherhood. The same symbolism reemerges later in Egypt where Isis, the great Mother, was sometimes depicted on tomb walls with outstretched wings to protect her people from harm. Birds with large eggs contained inside their bellies are a motif that is also found on pottery from Minoan Crete dating back to the second millennium BCE.

Most of the Neolithic Bird Goddesses are a combination of beaked heads and attributes characteristic of the female human body. Whether masked or not, these figurines all exhibit the symbols of the "Great Mother" according to Marija Gimbutas: chevrons, tri—lines, meanders, and streams. The chevron may have symbolized wings, the beak of a bird, or the genital triangle of the female womb. Gimbutas argues that the marking of an object with a chevron was a way of offering it to the Goddess. The different types of birds commonly affiliated with the "Great Mother" were water birds (ducks, geese, or herons), spring birds (cuckoos), and birds of prey (crows, owls, vultures). After the invention of pottery, vases and vessels frequently assumed the shape of water birds in Neolithic art.

The intrinsic symbolism of the Neolithic Bird Goddess is multilayered. Birds fly high in the skies. Not surprisingly, they came to be seen as connecting earthly life and the celestial realms. In Native American culture, birds were believed to be carriers of prayers and sacred knowledge – hence the term "soul bird." Birds also inhabit terrestrial rivers and lakes, and during the Neolithic period, the Goddess was also sometimes believed to be the source of the life—sustaining rain and the refreshing spring waters that welled up from beneath the ground. Water sustains plants, animals, and humans; it exemplifies the generative powers of the "Great Mother." Vessels and vases containing water or milk eventually became a prominent image of the Goddess herself, as Gimbutas has suggested. Neolithic vessels were frequently adorned with breasts, meanders and zigzags that imitated the fluid motion and non—linear patterns of water. These objects may also have symbolized the cosmic "Sky Mother," whose milk falls from her breasts as fertilizing rain. That may helps to explain why the sky in ancient Egypt came to represent the goddess Hathor, sometimes also referred to as the great "Cow of Heaven."

Another representation of the Bird Goddess as the bringer of life appears as a composite image that is half—woman, half—bird. This particularly interesting terracotta figurine – referred to as the "Self—Fertilizing Virgin Mother" by

Gimbutas – reveals a phallus—shaped neck and nurturing breasts that suggest an androgynous nature. This divine dual nature, the union of female and male attributes, is an expression of the all—encompassing sacred life force. Symbols of gender identification such as these have nothing to do with our modern and postmodern notions of sexuality, as Elinor Gadon argues in *The Once and Future Goddess*. Both the phallus and breasts can symbolize the creative life force. The concept of a dual primeval creator/creatrix is found in the cosmology and creation mythology of Native America and in ancient Egypt. This self—fertilizing primeval creator/creatrix encompassing both genders within his/her being then proceeds to produce the pairs of opposites, male and female, at a later time in evolution. Interestingly, these self—fertilizing and androgynous representations are consistent with the evolutionary reproduction process of the first microorganisms in water. The amoeba, for example, is gender—neutral and reproduces in a non—sexual way. Gender polarity is, relatively speaking, a late phenomenon in evolution.

Gadon reminds us that two seemingly contradictory notions coexisted in prehistoric religion. On the one hand, the "Great Goddess" encompassed all that was alive, both male and female, within her being, as exemplified in her representation as the "self—fertilizing Virgin Mother." On the other hand, with the domestication and breeding of animals, Neolithic people eventually came to understand the causal relationship between sexual intercourse and reproduction. As a result, the critical role of the male in engendering new life was ritually honored. The male sexual act eventually came to be seen as the plowing necessary for the seed to germinate within the fertile field that represented, among others, the body of the Goddess. To ensure the cyclical renewal of the crops, the Vegetation Goddess would mate with her young son—lover, the Year King, who had to be sacrificed, either literally or symbolically. Even though the image of the life—giving Goddess still predominates Neolithic art, it is nevertheless important to note that the symbols related to the sexes appear in a complementary relationship. Some of the most common symbols of the male are, for example, horned animals, most prominently bullhorns. Yet the bullhorns excavated in both houses and shrines at Çatalhöyük – a Neolithic settlement in south central Turkey (Anatolia) that dates back to the seventh millennium BCE – may also have served as objects of consecration to honor the Goddess. One of these shrines even depicts the Goddess herself giving birth to a young bull.

Neolithic conceptions of the Goddess portray her as both the sustainer of life and the harbinger of death as related to the cycle of life, death, and regeneration. In her representations as the "Mother of Death" she frequently loomed as a terrifying bird of prey, according to Marija Gimbutas. Yet contrary to modern and postmodern Western culture, death was not perceived as the end but rather as an integral part of the natural cycle during this prehistoric period. Just as new life emerges from decay, birth was simply viewed as part of a cyclical process that inevitably included death. The Goddess gave life, and she took life. This cyclical notion implied that the deceased were laid to rest in the earthly womb of the Goddess from which they would eventually reemerge at a later time. Gimbutas reminds us that the terms "tomb" and "womb" are interrelated.

The so—called "Vulture Shrine" at Çatalhöyük is the most impressive image of the Goddess of Death and Regeneration in Neolithic art, according to Cashford and

Baring. The walls of the shrine display vultures with outstretched wings swooping down on headless human corpses. The headless figures with their arms raised appear to be greeting the Goddess in her vulture form, possibly even flying with her in these other dimensions. Evidence exists that it was already a common practice during the Neolithic period to expose human corpses on outdoor platforms to vultures that would strip the bodies of their flesh, sparing only the bones that were eventually wrapped and buried underneath the family home. Gimbutas stresses that this procedure was considered necessary for the completion of the death process. She argues that the wall paintings of Çatalhöyük illustrate this so—called excarnation process. Perhaps the vulture was perceived as the compassionate "purifier" of the Goddess that disposed of the rotting flesh of the deceased. In fact, Baring and Cashford even argue that the process of feeding on carrion is a means of transforming that which is already dead back into life. Viewed in this particular context, the Goddess of Death and Birth is ultimately one. Life and death were perceived as complementary rather than as incompatible polar opposites.

Several thousand miles from the Near East, in the megalithic tombs of Western Europe, another raptor predominates in mortuary rituals. Our prehistoric ancestors carved the likeness of an owl, most prominently its eyes, into bones and majestic stone monuments. These megalithic "owl eyes" adorn necklaces and female breasts, sometimes they even appear in combination with the vulva. The superhuman qualities of the owl – its fantastic vision, mysterious stare, and nocturnal screams – likely evoked awe and a sense of mystery in our ancestors. This night bird naturally rules death and the underworld, yet it may also have been affiliated with the Goddess' role in regeneration, as Gimbutas opines.

The image of the Bird Goddess as the primordial Creatrix endures for some 25,000 years, from the thirtieth to the fifth millennium BCE. In many of the great civilizations after 3000 BCE, the relationship between the Goddess and the multi—faceted symbolism of the bird reemerges in numerous variations. For example, the figures of Isis and her sister Nephthys guard the sumptuous sarcophagus of the pharaoh as two long—winged protective birds. The dove – bird of epiphany symbolizing the Holy Spirit in Christianity – was sacred to the Sumerian goddess Inanna. And the swan and the goose are attributes of the Greek goddess Aphrodite. Moreover, the swan is a vehicle of the Hindu goddess Sarasvati in Indian iconography. In her aspect as the bringer of death and, eventually, regeneration, the Neolithic Bird Goddess reappears also as the Sumerian—Babylonian goddess Inanna—Ishtar flanked by owls. The owl – companion bird of the Greek goddess of wisdom Athena – continues to be the messenger of death throughout the period of classical Greece and beyond.

When the Neolithic Goddess appears as the "Mother of the Dead" she is usually carved from thin slabs of bone or ivory, and her body is stiff and rigid. Eventually, these figurines accompanied our ancestors into their graves. The arms of the "Goddess of Death" are folded tightly beneath her breasts, similar to the fetal position in which the bodies of the deceased were laid to rest. Unlike the usually lush and life—sustaining bodily attributes of the Paleolithic Mother figurines, the stiff white "Mother of the Dead" goddesses possess small breasts. Yet

Ceramic Neolithic female figurine, Cucuteni-Trypillian culture most of the wombs of these "stiff nudes," as Marija Gimbutas calls them, are marked by a giant sacred triangle that points toward the earth. Gimbutas suggests that the artist may have envisioned the universal womb, the inexhaustible source of life, to which the dead return to be born again. As the "Mother of the Dead," the Neolithic Goddess eventually accompanies her people during their transition from this life into the other dimensions – just as the Sumerian goddess Inanna would later embark on a voluntary journey to the underworld and Mother Mary would come to be seen as the intercessor for the souls of the deceased.

Neolithic Snake Goddess, about 4500 BCE
Crete Heraklion Museum

The Neolithic Serpent Goddess

The natural habitats of snakes are water and earth. Snakes hibernate in the ground during the winter and reemerge in spring. Further, snakes shed their skin periodically. Because of these characteristics, snakes came to symbolize immortality and eternal renewal. They were also sometimes thought to be embodiments of deceased ancestors, and the serpent's quick and fluid motion came to symbolize the dynamic power of water. In many mythologies, the serpent appears as the creative life source of the universe. Many cultures use the image of the serpent biting its tail and forming a closed circle – also referred to as the *uroboros* – to represent the primordial waters that encircle the earth. The snake was perceived as the creator and guardian of the spontaneous life energy that courses through the veins of a growing plant and coils around the belly of a pregnant mother. For example, the term "serpent power," that refers to the coiled up Goddess Kundalini at the base of the spine, likely derives from this idea. According to the yogic traditions of India, Kundalini is a subtle vital energy in our body that rises up the spine from the root chakra to the crown chakra, in a motion similar to that of a serpent. If awakened, this subtle energy representing the Goddess activates the liberating power of consciousness that leads to illumination. Because of its coiling motion and its capability to regenerate itself by shedding its skin, images of the serpent represented the Goddess' power of regeneration, particularly her power to restore life to the dead. The serpent's cyclical pattern of hibernation may also have suggested the awakening of life from the temporary paralysis of death.

Many Neolithic sculptures of the Snake Goddess portray her as sitting or squatting. Her body is commonly adorned with stripes and spirals, while her arms and legs are represented as snakes or as entwined by them. The head appears in either human form or as a snake; sometimes the goddess is masked and wears a crown. As with the Bird Goddess, our Neolithic ancestors affiliated specific symbols with the Snake Goddess such as, for example, the spiral or the zigzag that emulate the serpent's movements. The spiral, an abstract derivative of the snake, is a very popular motif in the art of prehistoric Europe, and is symbolically related to the labyrinth.

The labyrinth represents the journey to the centre that is our true Self. This journey leads to death, followed by rebirth into another state of being and relating to the world. Some of the earliest spiral rock engravings dating back to the Paleolithic period are reminders of our ancestor's unceasing preoccupation with the spiraling patterns of the universe, which was, coincidentally, envisioned as a giant cosmic serpent. Today, with the progress of modern science, the same pattern is known to rule the galaxies at a macro level, and the double helix spiral of the DNA molecule at a micro level. The spiral is hence an archetypal symbol emerging from natural processes. It is associated with both the energies of creation and destruction. Yet the same spiraling motion also underlies the evolution of human culture and consciousness. Along with all the other universal phenomena, value systems that shape our worldviews evolve as well, as the previously mentioned theory of human development referred to as Spiral Dynamics demonstrates. The late Clare Graves, a pioneer in the field of developmental psychology, noticed that new worldviews and values systems emerge to assist a particular culture to adapt to new challenges and changing life conditions. This process does not generally follow a linear path; it evolves, and like a spiral staircase it circles back on itself, according to Graves. With each revolution, new values systems arise that reach a more complex level in an effort to resolve the challenges created by the previous stage. The spiral thus clearly reflects the creative dynamic principle by which new manifestations transcend, yet also partly include, previous manifestations.

The spiral as an archetypal symbol of birth and creation finds expression in another representation of the Snake Goddess that dates back to the fifth millennium BCE and originates in Thessaly, Greece. Snakes are coiled over the body of an enthroned goddess who holds her child in her arms. According to Cashford and Baring, this may be one of the earliest images of the Snake Goddess found in cultures that range from prehistoric Mesopotamia to the Indus River Valley civilization of modern—day Pakistan. The umbilical cord that connects the child to its mother has the form of two intertwined snakes similar to the double helix spiral of the DNA. To this day, the image of the double serpent is also known as a symbol of the medical profession, which can be traced to the Aesclepian temple healing tradition of the pre—modern Mediterranean world (the tradition was named after the Greek healing god, Aesclepias).

In many of the later emerging great civilizations such as Minoan Crete, snakes are depicted as spiraling around vases and coiled over pregnant bellies, buttocks, and phalluses. As the dynamic cosmic principle of the inexhaustible life energy, they undulate between the moon and the stars. The enduring power of serpent symbolism is expressed in another prehistoric sculpture from the Pyrenees that shows the "Great Mother" giving birth to a snake and suckling it. In the mythology of Mesoamerica, snake symbolism appears in association with the great Earth goddess Coatlicue, who is also referred to as the "Lady of the Serpent Skirt." The Aztec god Quetzalcoatl was represented as a feathered serpent, symbolizing the sacred union of heaven (bird) and earth (snake). In order to be reborn, this archetypal savior—hero first had to die. A last example expressing the ambiguity of snake symbolism and its affiliation with both renewal and death is seen in the mythological figure of Medusa, a monstrous winged creature who has snakes in her hair. The ancient Greeks believed that blood from Medusa's snaky hair contained magic properties that could both destroy and create. The first venomous drop from her hair caused instant death; the second, from her veins, was thought to bring rebirth and life.

The "Great Mother" of the prehistoric period is complex. Sometimes she appears as hybrid: half human, half animal. In addition to manifestations as a bird and as a serpent, the Goddess, according to Marjia Gimbutas, is also affiliated with the frog and the hedgehog (both symbols of regeneration), the deer and the bear (birthing and nursing), the bee (renewal) and the butterfly (transformation and regeneration). She was the pregnant "Earth Mother" watching over Paleolithic cave sanctuaries; and in the Neolithic period, she was the "Vegetation Goddess" who governed the seasonal cycles and represented the abundance and fertility necessary for the germination, sprouting, growing, and ripening of crops.

Goddess—Centered Spiritual Beliefs as a Celebration of Life

A theme notably absent from Neolithic art is imagery idealizing warfare, cruelty, and domination. This stands in sharp contrast to the art emerging in subsequent civilizations after 3000 BCE, as Riane Eisler and other feminist scholars have repeatedly stressed. In prehistoric art, no images of battle scenes or "noble warriors" exist, nor do we find signs of "heroic" conquests in which captives of war are treated brutally and/or held as slaves. Unlike our modern and postmodern times, no separation between the secular and the sacred existed in prehistoric, and well into historic, times. Religious observance and beliefs were fully integrated into everyday life. But to argue that people who worshiped the Goddess were deeply "religious" misses the point. As Riane Eisler puts it succinctly: "If the central image was a woman giving birth and not, as in our time, a man dying on a cross, it would not be unreasonable to infer that life and the love of life – rather than death and the fear of death – were dominant in society as well as art." Gimbutas also argues that the religious symbolism of prehistory, and the worship of the Goddess as the great Creatrix, reflects most likely a *matrilineal* system. In matrilineal societies, descent and inheritance are traced through the mother. One of the indicators providing evidence of this theory are the numerous mother—daughter images found in prehistoric art, while the image of the archetypal father, so prevalent in later times, is basically non—existent. Gimbutas points out that the archaeological evidence leaves little doubt that women played key roles in the societies of "Old Europe" that were run exclusively by a council of women from the leading clans, headed eventually by a priestess—queen. According to Gimbutas, men performed skilled roles as artisans and engaged in trade, but women were the ones who performed most sacred rites and governed society.

Yet, while other feminist scholars who are critical of Gimbutas' conclusions concede that she has provided us with an enormous amount of intriguing images and artifacts, they nevertheless question her overall interpretative framework. One of the main points of contention voiced by her critics is that Gimbutas attributes exclusive female leadership to prehistoric societies while, at the same time, insisting that she is talking about completely *egalitarian* societies in which women *and* men were fully equal. This position has been criticized by other feminist archaeologists and scholars for its inconsistency. According to Rosemary Radford Ruether, even in "existing matrilineal societies, major spheres of power are given to males, even if their leadership roles are derived from their mothers. No society gives women all the public power roles in government and religion."[4] Radford Ruether points out that relative egalitarianism is not necessarily an indicator that a society is matrilineal and matrilocal. With that said, feminist scholars basically agree that prehistoric cultures were *not* matriarchal, a term that implies the domination of men by women. We can tentatively conclude that prehistoric society was egalitarian with no marked distinctions based on either class or sex. In this context, Riane Eisler reminds us that Neolithic imagery representing the relationship between the genders reflects an attitude in which linking, rather than ranking, appears to be the norm.

While the Sacred Feminine in its numerous manifestations clearly predominates Neolithic art and religion, the male principle also plays a vital role. The male deity, commonly represented as a young man or a horned animal, likely affirmed and strengthened the forces of the active and creative female principle. No gender was subordinate to the other – by complementing each other, their powers were doubled. The fusion of the female and the male principles is expressed most beautifully in the ritualistic sacred marriage. This ritual eventually originated in the Neolithic, yet it was celebrated for thousands of years well into the classical times of the great civilizations in which the ceremony survived as the *hieros gamos*.

---

[4] Radford Ruether, *Goddesses and the Divine Feminine*, p. 25.

INANNA/ISHTAR IN ANCIENT MESOPOTAMIA

Inanna and Dumuzi

The Sacred Marriage Rite of Inanna and Dumuzi

S acred rituals uniting the female and the male may have taken place in prehistoric times, although little archaeological evidence exists. A Neolithic terra—cotta statuette, the "Gumelnita Lovers," from a site in southern Romania (c. 5000 BCE), represents a man and a woman tenderly embracing each other and may have portrayed participants in a ritualistic sacred marriage.

The earliest descriptions of ceremonial sexual intercourse, dating to the early third millennium BCE, have been passed down from the written records of ancient Mesopotamia, the land between the Tigris and Euphrates rivers in modern—day Iraq. Ritualistic duties fell to a few elected individuals such as the queen and king or the high priestess and high priest, who performed the marriage rites on behalf of their subjects (in earliest times, the high priest and the king were likely identical).

In ancient Sumer, the king was regarded as human and, at the same time, as the embodiment of the mythological Dumuzi (the name means "faithful son"), also referred to as the "Vegetation God" or the "Divine Shepherd." The kings of Sumer were perceived as shepherds because of the role they played as servants of the gods and custodians of the land and its produce. Originally viewed as mortals, the kings of Mesopotamia eventually became deified over time because of their participation in ritualistic sacred marriage. In this rite, the king as Dumuzi was wedded ritually to the high priestess, who was believed to be an incarnation of the goddess Inanna/Ishtar, the "Queen of Heaven" – who was thought to descend to earth for this special occasion (in Babylonia, the Sumerian goddess Inanna was later fused with her Semitic counterpart Ishtar). Though there were variations, the essence of this sacred rite remained constant through the centuries. The ritual was performed at the time of the autumn equinox, which coincided with the beginning of the New Year when the earth awakened and the winter crop was planted.

As part of the preparations for the rite, songs of courtship were exchanged between Inanna and Dumuzi. These hymns are a testimony of the exuberant passion aroused between the Goddess and her consort that also held the promise of a plentiful harvest. Inanna cries out in delight in expectation of sexual pleasure, using the metaphors of the plowman plowing a field ripe for planting:

"My vulva, the horn (of abundance),
is full of eagerness like the young moon.
My untilled land lies fallow.
Who will plow my vulva?
Who will plow my high field?
Who will plow my wet ground?"

Dumuzi eagerly replies:

"Great Lady, the king will plow your vulva
I, Dumuzi the King, will plow your vulva."

Inanna:

"Then plow my vulva, man of my heart!"
At the king's lap stood the rising cedar
Plants grew high by their side.
Grains grew high by their side.
Gardens flourished luxuriantly.

Inanna rejoices:

"He has sprouted; he has burgeoned;
He is lettuce planted by the water.
My well—stocked garden of the plain,
My barley growing high in its furrow

My apple tree which bears fruit up to its crown,

My honey—man, my honey—man sweetens me always...

He is the one my womb loves best."

These songs of courtship between Inanna and Dumuzi reveal that the primary purpose of ritualistic sacred marriage was to ensure the cyclical renewal of nature and an abundant harvest for the people of ancient Mesopotamia. The role of the male in this rite is that of a consort to the Goddess. As already established within the context of Neolithic art, the archetypal masculine plays an important part in the process of becoming, yet it does not actually hold new life as does the female body. Inanna was considered to be an embodiment of the fields yielding grain, while Dumuzi was believed to possess the fertilizing power that made the plants burgeon. In these songs of courtship, Inanna rejoices in her sexuality and participation in sexual union. However she does not extol motherhood, childcare, or weaving which are all traditionally affiliated with the archetypal feminine. It is important to note that it was agricultural prosperity, *not* a human child, which was the anticipated outcome of this sacred union. Inanna's sexuality was celebrated as non—monogamous and extrafamilial – and not linked to her reproductive capacity.

Another Sumerian poem, equally evocative of sexual imagery, reveals the close bond between the priest, shepherd, king, and bull symbolism. The divine shepherd Dumuzi is referred to as a "wild bull." Dumuzi, the husband and son—lover of Inanna, is repeatedly called the "Bull of Heaven." Anne Baring and Jules Cashford remind us that the image of the bull played an important role in Sumerian mythology as well as in all other pre—modern Mediterranean and Near Eastern cultures.

In contrast to the public display and joyous celebration of Inanna's sexuality in ancient Mesopotamia, it is interesting to note that most traditional forms of organized religion subsequently taught (and they still do so at the time of this writing) that sexuality is an impediment to spiritual progress and that the body is a potential "reservoir of sin" that has to be transcended. From a broader evolutionary perspective, sexuality as a basic biological function has no moral dimension; it is neither "good" nor "bad." Rather, sexuality is a neutral force that serves a fundamental evolutionary purpose, namely, it leads to procreation. Of course, sexuality can be expressed in numerous ways, considered positive or negative depending on the prevailing moral law codes of a particular society or culture. Examples of a positive expression of the sexual impulse are authentic love relationships between conscious and mature adults – while rape and child abuse are clearly a negative expression. Yet sexual abuse as such cannot be blamed on the human body, rather, this behavior comes from the motivations of a troubled and deluded personality. The sexual impulse itself is beyond the moral rules that constitute an integral part of the law codes found in all religious systems.

As part of the preparations for the ritualistic sacred marriage, the king visited Inanna's temple with the appropriate offerings, hoping to earn her favors. In addition to the prospect of prosperity and agricultural abundance, the ritualistic marriage of the Goddess with the king was also a way of validating the king's rise to power and a means of legitimizing his authority for another year. The kings of ancient Mesopotamia claimed the throne not through direct inheritance or succession but by divine election. As the courting bridegroom and the son—lover of Inanna, the king had been consecrated, winning her endorsement for another year of rule after which the ritual had to be re—enacted. This clearly shows how the rite – the first in recorded history – served as an instrument of official state policy in ancient Mesopotamia. Not surprisingly, the populace equally rejoiced in the preparations for the festivities.

People brought sumptuous offerings to the temple of Inanna: sheep, butter, dates, fruits of all kind, beer, wine and more. The rite then took place in the bridal chamber of Inanna's temple. The sacred marriage bed, fashioned from the mythological Tree of Life, was carefully prepared. The Tree of Life – a universal symbol that represents the world axis – appears also in a very ancient Sumerian seal dating back to c. 2500 BCE. In addition to the Tree of Life, this seal depicts the Goddess facing her consort, the Shepherd—King. A serpent rises on its coils next to the Goddess. The imagery of this scene clearly evokes the well—known plot in Eden that was to be given so different a meaning in Genesis hundreds of years later. This seal may be one of the oldest Sumerian images of the ritualistic sacred marriage to survive the passage of time.

The culminating events of the rite are described in hymns of praise. Over the sacred marriage bed, a specially prepared coverlet was spread. Inanna was washed, soaped, perfumed with precious ointments and laid on the bed. The king then proceeded to the "holy lap" and blissfully bedded with the Goddess. The following day, a rich banquet took place in the large reception hall of the royal palace. The entire community engaged in much eating and drinking, listening to music and singing as the people of Sumer paraded before the divine couple sitting side by side on their thrones.

Inanna was hence not only viewed as a goddess who guaranteed the continued welfare of her community, but also as the source of the king's power. Her participation in this sacred union was an expression of the power through which the Divine Feminine touched the highest political ranks of the human world, the realm of the kings. Through marriage to Inanna, kings were exalted, put on the throne, and vested with the powers to rule. Yet in the end, kings never truly became immortal in ancient Mesopotamia. They shared the common fate of the human condition: death. Only through marriage to Inanna could kings be temporarily like the gods, sharing in their power and glory.

How was the goddess Inanna portrayed in Sumerian mythology? One of the most striking aspects is that Inanna never acts as a nubile bride who becomes a dutiful and submissive wife. In fact, in Sumero—Babylonian narratives, she is portrayed as impetuous, ambitious, and ready to fight for her own prerogatives. Clay tablets dating to the late third millennium BCE show the Goddess with signs of her ruling power and weapons emerging from her shoulders, her foot resting on the back of a lion. Other representations show her as a "Goddess of War" who rides ahead of a war chariot and even brings captives to the king. Inanna can supply both political power and military victory to the king.

These depictions of the Goddess engaged in brutal conquest and warfare may seem surprising, especially in light of the predominantly life—affirming representations of the Great Mother in the Paleolithic and Neolithic periods. Yet, the emergence of numerous city—states in Sumer in the early third millennium BCE led to continuous warfare and fierce competition among the city—states. Clearly, the historical—cultural context needs to be taken into consideration when interpreting the specific role and function of Inanna as a "Goddess of War." In *Rebirth of the Goddess,* feminist theologian Carol Christ argues that images of armed goddesses reflect the transformation of earlier goddesses by patriarchal warrior societies that are ruled by warrior kings, as was the case in ancient Mesopotamia. In contrast, the great Goddess of the prehistoric period was never armed, although she did most likely appear as the Taker of Life in her manifestation as a vulture, as we have established.

Sacred Marriage Rites and "Temple Prostitution"

One more aspect of these sacred marriage rites requires clarification. Throughout history, temple priestesses in premodern cultures of the Near East have often been referred to as "temple prostitutes," mostly by male scholars. Can this characterization withstand critical inquiry? Do we have evidence that cultic ritualistic sex was widely practiced in ancient Mesopotamia? In *Goddesses and the Divine Feminine,* Rosemary Radford—Ruether cautions that the ritualistic sacred marriage between the high priestess/Inanna and the king does not imply that sacred prostitution was practiced in Sumero—Babylonian temples. Radford—Ruether points out that this notion likely derives from the Greek historian Herodotus' questionable description of sacred prostitution in a Babylonian temple, which has misled (mostly male) interpreters to assume that "temple prostitution" was characteristic of both ancient Mesopotamian and Canaanite fertility rites. This notion was certainly reinforced by the Hebrew prophets of the first millennium BCE who repeatedly used the metaphor of ancient Israel being an "unfaithful wife" to God, a "harlot" engaged in promiscuous sexual acts, "prostituting" herself to foreign powers by adopting polytheistic fertility cults.

As long as temple priestesses were the carriers of life—
enhancing and mysterious powers, these powers could
not be claimed by the God of the Jews, viewed as the one
and only creator. Hebrew scriptures do mention temple
priestesses in Jerusalem, at least until the destruction of
the First Temple and the ensuing period of the Babylonian
Exile (587 BCE). With that said, however, the notion of
"sacred prostitution" remains highly problematic and
does not withstand the criteria of historical inquiry.
Radford Ruether concludes that, "studies of the extensive
personnel records of ancient temples show no evidence
of any practice of sacred prostitution. Although ordinary
prostitutes were common in all these (Near Eastern)
societies...there is no evidence that sexual orgies were
a part of official temple worship or that a class of
priestesses performed as sacred prostitutes."[5] Aside from
the arguments that can be raised against or in favor of
ritualistic sacred sex, it is essential to emphasize, as most
feminist scholars have done, that ancient Near Eastern
priestesses were *not* prostitutes in the modern sense of
the term because they did not sell their sexual services. If
ritualistic sex was practiced, its role was solely sacred.

Anne Baring and Jules Cashford remind us that the
ritualistic sacred marriage symbolized the union of moon
and sun, heaven and earth. As the union of moon and sun,
the mythic narrative of the Goddess and her God—King
was clearly exalted into cosmic dimensions. Inanna, the
"Queen of Heaven," claimed as her characteristic symbolic
attributes the moon and Venus, the morning and evening
star. This may have given rise to the image of the eight—
pointed star and the stylized rosette with eight petals.
In some Mesopotamian seals, Inanna/Ishtar is shown

---

[5] Radford Ruether, *Goddesses and the Divine Feminine*, p. 82.

with numerous stars that encircle her head, and she
eventually came to personify the zodiac. The same cosmic
imagery reemerges later in Christianity with the Virgin
Mary symbolically adorned with a halo of golden stars.
In addition to the moon and Venus, it was in particular
the star Sirius that held great symbolic significance in the
ancient Near East and was, among others, affiliated with
Inanna/Ishtar in Mesopotamia and with Isis in Egypt.

Sacred Marriage Rites and the Soul's Union with the Divine

Ritualistic sacred marriage was celebrated in numerous
variations across the world's cultures. In Egypt the rite
was performed in temples dedicated to Isis and Osiris.
We find the invocation of similar imagery and symbolism
in the biblical *Song of Songs*, one of the most beautiful
expressions of sacred marriage literature passed down
through the ages. Talmudic tradition assigns authorship
of *The Song of Songs* – a bridal song – to the young king
Solomon. Anne Baring and Jules Cashford argue that this
sacred text relates to the imagery of the great Goddess, who
may have been Solomon's consort in a sacred marriage rite
similar to the one celebrated in ancient Mesopotamia. The
vividness of the sexual imagery and the rich description
of the earth's plentiful fruits suggest that its origin may
not be Judaic, but may go back to a time when the earth
and sexuality were *not* split off from the divine. The great
Jewish mystic Rabbi Akiba (c. 45—135 CE) interpreted
The Song of Songs as an allegory of the love of the Jews for
God. Jewish esoteric traditions such as Kabbalah drew
heavily on the imagery of bride and groom in their mystical
writings. Sacred marriage was seen as an expression of
the union between the archetypal masculine and feminine
aspects of God – with the feminine aspect also referred
to as the *Shekhinah* – and between the soul as related to

the masculine, and wisdom as related to the feminine. In addition, the Jewish Sabbath is sometimes personified as a "bride" and welcomed with the same yearning with which one prepares for a wedding ceremony.

Bridal symbolism and imagery emerged also in the Christian tradition. The biblical *Book of Revelation* informs us that after all evil has been vanquished by Christ, the New Jerusalem, pictured as a "celestial bride," will descend from heaven to merge with her bridegroom in divine union (Rev. 21:2). However the explicit sensuality of *The Song of Songs* became entirely spiritualized as a mental love in the Christian tradition. Throughout the ages, Christian monastic interpreters insisted that *The Song of Songs* was conducive only to those who had purged themselves of all temptations and desires of the flesh. One of the early church fathers, Origen, who lived in Alexandria in the third century CE, argued that *The Song of Songs* points through the veil of allegory to two different aspects of the marriage between the divine and humanity: the marriage between Christ and the Church (*ecclesia*), and the union between Christ and the individual soul (*anima*). Origen made sure to banish from the reader's mind any attention to the lush eroticism found in the actual text of *The Song of Songs*. For him, the explicitly erotic language was a mere external veil that concealed the true spiritual meaning of the text. Origen concluded that the love referred to in the poetry was not of a bodily nature but exclusively spiritual in its essence.

While the Church eventually came to claim the position of the redeemed "Bride of Christ," the sacred marriage theme was over time gradually transformed by Christian mystics into a metaphor that reflected the profound esoteric experience in which the awakened soul yearned to be united with the divine. The great German medieval mystic, Mechthild of Magdeburg (the dates of her birth and death are estimated to be c. 1208—1294), experienced her yearning soul as "God's lover." For her, the creation of the soul by God was an expression of the primordial work of divine love. Contrary to the orthodox image of God as self—sufficient, the divine is incomplete without the soul as "beloved," according to Mechthild. God's intense love for the soul is depicted with explicit eroticism in her work. In the manner of a courtly lover, God is depicted bending his knee to Lady Soul. The bride clothes herself in virtues in preparation for the ensuing love dance. But when she enters the bridal chamber, her divine lover bids her strip off her clothes. When the soul becomes "naked," perfectly conformed to God, external practices of virtues need no longer come between God and the soul. God surrenders himself to the soul, and the soul surrenders herself to God in a love union that anticipates eternal life without death. In her writings, Mechthild repeatedly emphasized God's infinite desire to be "loved from the heart." Yet, the love relationship with God is not just blissful ecstasy for Mechthild. Mostly, it incurs pain and suffering, that is, a pain rooted in human estrangement from the divine, bodily finitude, and the frustrations that result from being fundamentally misunderstood in her way of living.

Chakrasamvara Embracing Vajravarahi

Male and Female Archetypes and Subtle Energies within Conceptions of the Divine

An expression of the archetypal mystical union of the feminine and masculine is found in the iconography of Vajrayana, tantric Tibetan Buddhism. For example, the blue—colored Chakrasamvara, one of the three supreme beings worshipped by the Gelug order, is shown embracing his female consort, the red—bodied Vajravarahi. The two figures, merging into each other in supreme and blissful ecstasy, embody the endless cycle of samsaric rebirths and the ultimate identity of time and eternity. Moreover, Tibetan Buddhism teaches that the entire spectrum of consciousness correlates with a specific type of *prana* that can be roughly defined as embodied vital energy. These correlations are prominently expounded in the yogic chakra system.

Seven major chakras, or subtle energy centers, exist. Each of these chakras is related to one of the stages of consciousness, starting with the root chakra at the base of the spine, and going all the way up to the thousand—petalled lotus chakra at the crown of the head. The first three chakras – concerned primarily with food, sexuality, and power – correspond roughly to what integral theory refers to as the egocentric or preconventional stage. Chakras four and five, as an expression of heart—centered connection and communication, have an ethnocentric, conventional gravity center. And chakras six and seven, as related to the highest psycho—spiritual faculties, have a worldcentric and even cosmocentric orientation transcending the concerns that are exclusively focused on the family, the tribe, and the nation. Once the sixth and the seventh chakras have been fully activated, we care for humanity as a whole and for all other—than—human life forms as well. The chakra system clearly demonstrates how every stage of consciousness corresponds to a specific type of vital energy.

Two types of vital energy stand out: prana in its small form on the one hand, and prana in its more extensive form on the other. Prana in its small form orchestrates primarily the act of sexual union between two organisms, may they be human or other—than—human life forms. In its more extensive form, prana goes beyond the desire to merge with just one partner. This type of vital energy unites one sentient organism with the entire universe in a profound nondual experience that can be tremendously liberating, because it offers deliverance from the small egoic self and its corresponding sexual cravings and selfish attachments. The tantric traditions of the East hence emphasize that liberation implies not just a shift in consciousness from small self to true Self, but also a shift in vital energetic patterns from "small prana" to "big prana," as Ken Wilber puts it. As "big prana," sexual energy has the potential to serve as a vehicle to union with the divine.

Another expression of the ever—evolving interplay between the archetypal feminine and the archetypal masculine is the *yin/yang* symbol in Chinese Daoism. Dark (yin/feminine) and light (yang/masculine) form a sacred circle with each containing a part of the other's essence within itself. Yin and yang are not divided by a straight line, which would create an absolute polarity. Instead, they are separated by an S curve, suggesting that the distinction is fluid, alternating, and continually at play. We understand yin and yang to be complementary. The combined archetypal polarities create life – together they form a harmonious universe.

In this context, we must be careful to avoid using stereotypes. The Jungian—influenced dichotomy of distinct "feminine" and "masculine" qualities is somewhat arbitrary, and subject to personal and socio—cultural conditioning. The terms "feminine" and "masculine" are *not* synonymous with "male" and "female" – though they carry connotations that are so ingrained in our psyches that we consciously and unconsciously react to them with gender prejudices. In addition, women and men are complex, each with a range of potentialities. The archetypal sacred marriage can hence serve as a metaphor for the integration of the masculine and the feminine, god and goddess, and for all the possible polarities within the self. In *Dancing in the Flames*, author and Jungian analyst Marion Woodman points to the necessity of both men and women integrating the well—differentiated masculine and well—differentiated feminine within themselves. In her book *In a Different Voice*, psychologist Carol Gilligan talks about the different stages or structures of moral development (from selfish/egocentric to care/ethnocentric to universal/worldcentric to integrated/cosmocentric) through which both men and women will eventually evolve. At the fourth and most evolved stage, the masculine and the feminine aspects in each of us tends to become integrated, according to Gilligan's research. This means that individuals start to tune into both the masculine and feminine modes within themselves.

The union expressed within archetypal sacred marriage is not restricted to heterosexual relationships. What matters are the qualities brought to any form of relationship, including relationships between family members, friends, and straight or gay individuals. Both men and women have internal opposites to integrate. Just as this integration should occur within the individual self as part of a healthy and balanced maturation, it needs to occur in a collective context, within institutions, organizations, and governments, to stimulate our social maturation on a broader scale. A wholesome balance of the archetypal masculine and the archetypal feminine is at the heart of ritualistic sacred marriage and the multi—faceted imagery and symbolism that exists in so many variations and cultures.

The Descent of Inanna to the Underworld

The goddess Inanna is also exalted in her identification with another mythic cycle central to the kingship ideology of ancient Sumer – her descent to, and subsequent return from, the underworld. In this context, the question arises: How did the people of ancient Mesopotamia envision the realm of the dead? Two different notions stand out. During the late Sumerian period, and particularly in the Babylonian and Assyrian civilizations, people came to regard the underworld as a gloomy and fearful place that was inhabited by terrifying demons and evil spirits that could seize upon the souls of humans. This frightening vision did not inspire hope or trust in an afterlife. Over time, death in ancient Mesopotamia was viewed as final, and not as a transitory rite of passage between two dimensions as, for example, was seen in the optimistic conception of the afterlife in ancient Egypt.

In the older and more complete Sumerian version of this narrative, Inanna voluntarily chooses to embark on a journey to the underworld. She desires to add the realm of the dead, ruled by her sister Ereshkigal, to her realms of power as the "Queen of Heaven and Earth." Inanna descends into the great unknown, the dark womb of the inner earth, in search of the wisdom that it holds. At each of the seven gates of the underworld, she is allowed to pass through only after being divested of one of her divine powers and worldly prerogatives. When Inanna, the Goddess of Life, embarks on this archetypal journey into the depths of her own being, she has to reconcile herself with the phenomena of loss and death. Naked and bowed low, she finally enters the throne room of her sister Ereshkigal, who displays hostility toward her because of Inanna's rich life experience. Ereshkigal gazes at her sister with the "eye of death." The mythic narrative tells us that Inanna then hangs like a rotting corpse on a hook for three days. This scene evokes the moon's symbolic death as the "dark moon," before reappearing again after three days, initiating a new lunar cycle. During these three days, Inanna gains essential insights into the full circle of existence.

When the goddess Inanna doesn't return to earth, her messengers approach the other deities for assistance. Enki, the god of wisdom, is the only one who understands what is at stake, namely, that civilization in Sumer could regress to a primitive stage if Inanna is not rescued from the realm of the dead. After all, it was she who originally brought the gift of civilization to Mesopotamia. Enki devises a way to rescue Inanna that restores her life and allows her to return and assume her rightful place as the "Queen of Heaven and Earth." Now the goddess represents the unification of three worlds: heaven, earth, and underworld. The narrative of her descent is a powerful metaphor of the emergence of life from death and light from darkness.

An impressive terracotta relief dating from the late third millennium BCE portrays Inanna as the goddess of the "Great Above and the Great Below." She is crowned with four horned tiers and her taloned feet rest on two tamed lions. Inanna displays a female human body, yet she is winged. Two owls stand sentinel at her left and right, suggesting affiliation with the Neolithic bird goddess. Later, the same symbolism reemerged in the figure of Lilith in Hebrew mythology. Lilith may have been a distorted image of the great Sumerian goddess because she was in biblical times not only referred to as "night owl" and "demon" but was also believed to be a harbinger of the powers of death, most prominently affecting women in childbirth. Unlike Lilith, the winged Inanna flanked by owls and lions does not terrify, but rather inspires with the majesty of her presence in her role as the great Goddess of the three worlds of heaven, earth, and the underworld.

The "Burney Relief" representation of
Sumerian Goddess Innana

The Descent of Dumuzi to the Underworld

After returning to the land of the living, Inanna must
abide by the laws of the underworld and provide a
suitable substitute. In the meantime Dumuzi, sitting on
her throne, enjoys the powers of kingship. He hasn't
even noticed that Inanna has left, nor does he show
any compassion for the ordeal she has endured during
her journey through the realm of death. In response to
Dumuzi's indifference, Inanna decides that her husband
should be her surrogate. Just as Inanna had to abandon
her wordly prerogatives at each gate, Dumuzi, too, must
divest himself of his earthly powers. It is only through
the self—sacrifice of Dumuzi's sister that the king's fate

is modified. He only has to be in the underworld between the harvests, when the fields are barren. He is allowed to ascend again, and can live on the earthly plane during the remainder of the year when new life is restored.

The narrative of Inanna's descent to the underworld is related to the myth of the dying and rising vegetation god Dumuzi, the "Divine Shepherd." As the vital principle of the agricultural cycle, Dumuzi dies when the searing heat of summer initiates a long drought during which the populace anxiously awaits the New Year rains that will initiate growth. As king of Sumer, Dumuzi is identified with the harvest of the land. Yet, as the mortal consort of the great Goddess, he must be sacrificed – either literally or symbolically – for the earth to be renewed. Through his sacrifice, his sacred powers are renewed in spring when he is believed to return from the underworld. Inanna and Dumuzi's marriage during the remainder of the year reflects the mystery of sexual union that was believed to ensure fertility and abundant crops.

Myths of the Sacrificed King, Sacrificial Lamb, Good Shepherd, and Horned God

The mythology of the sacrificed king lies at the heart of the Christian story. Interestingly, Jesus Christ is referred to as a "Sacrificial Lamb" and "Good Shepherd" in the Gospels. This is similar to the mythic conception of Dumuzi as the "Divine Shepherd" and consort of the great Goddess. Moreover, most of the mythology and symbolism of the sacrificed god—king has endured the centuries in the storehouse of folkloric tales that reemerged in numerous guises. Another such figure is the so—called "Green Man." His face gazes out from the midst of carved foliage on Gothic cathedral screens, pulpits, and choir stalls. Similar to the vegetation god Dumuzi, the Green

Man symbolizes death and rebirth in the natural cycle. He embodies the fertilizing life force upon which agricultural societies depend. Another example is the Greek god Dionysus, also known as Bacchus in Rome, whose head is adorned with grapes and vine leaves. Dionysus is the god of joyful liberating ecstasy and wild intoxicating frenzy. Over time, he eventually became an embodiment of all that was later suppressed in the collective psyche of Western civilization, most prominently the sexual creative life force. Death during the winter season and subsequent rebirth in spring is also a motif in the mythic narrative of Dionysus.

The Green Man was symbolically affiliated with the "Horned God," called Herne in the Celtic tradition. The Horned God is usually represented with the body of a man, yet his feet are depicted as hooves, and his head is crowned with either horns or antlers. The Horned God is equally related to Dumuzi, who was sometimes also referred to as "wild bull" in ancient Mesopotamia. In Roman mythology, the Horned God made his appearance as the noisy and merry god, Pan, commonly depicted as part—animal with horns, hooves, and a hairy body (the term "panic" derives from him). Because of his appearance and the sexual connotations, the Horned God serves as a prominent example of a pagan deity who became anathema in Christianity and was, in fact, even vilified in the figure of the "devil" who, coincidentally, shares similar physical attributes.

The Journey of the Sacrificial God / Consort of the Goddess

The archetypal journey of the god – whether he is referred to as the Horned God, Green Man, or Year King because of the annual seasonal cycle – basically

follows the four solar celebrations of Spring Equinox,
Midsummer, Autumn Equinox, and Yule that coincide
with the cardinal points of East, South, West, and North.
The four Celtic festivals – Beltane, Lammas, Hallowe'en,
and Candlemas – are placed between the cardinal points.
These festivals celebrate the natural cycle of the seasons
and also constitute an integral part of Wiccan rituals
today, just as they did in pre—modern times. The Spring
Equinox is the time when the mating between the goddess
and the young phallic god takes place. Beltane, or May
Eve, welcomes the summer and celebrates the marriage
between goddess and god. In midsummer, the god comes
into his maturity as king and assumes full responsibility
for the land. Lammas, in autumn, celebrates the harvest.
Early autumn is also the time when the sacrifice of the
god is required for the purpose of fertilizing the land.
Moreover, his sacrifice liberates him to conquer the realm
of the underworld and, eventually, the wisdom it holds.
As the "Dark Lord," the god returns from the underworld
at the time of the Autumn Equinox to reclaim his queen,
the goddess, and take her with him to his underworld
kingdom. One of the most popular festivals, Hallowe'en
or Samhain, is the feast of the dead, when the worlds of
matter and spirit draw close to one another and the dead
may pass to and fro through the veils. And finally, in the
midst of winter, the birth of the young Sun God, the child
of promise, is celebrated at Yule, when light increasingly
starts to replace darkness until they eventually reach a
perfect balance at the time of the Spring Equinox. The
light replacing the darkness is also the central theme
of the Christmas celebration around the time of the
Winter Solstice.

The connections between the archetypal journey of the
sacrificial god and consort of the goddess on the one
hand, and the seasonal cycle of agriculture on the other

hand, are apparent in the sacrifice of the "Year King"
at the time of the harvest, the absence of plant growth
during the dark winter months, and the return of the
young god in spring that heralds the joyful news that life
is reborn from death. This annual cycle of the vegetation
god's journey provided hence the mythic basis for the
death and resurrection drama that was ritually celebrated
for centuries throughout the entire pre—Christian
Mediterranean world. In this context, the Great Goddess
may be understood as the eternal cycle representing
the unity of life and death as a single process, while
the Young God – perceived as her mortal form in time
manifest as plant, animal, or human being – is subject to
a cyclical process of birth, flowering, decay, death, and
subsequent rebirth.

ISIS: GODDESS OF A THOUSAND NAMES

Isis in Egyptian Cosmology

"In the Beginning there was Isis: Oldest of the Old, She was the Goddess from whom all Becoming Arose..."[6] This hymn from fourteenth century BCE Thebes, praises the goddess Isis as the matrix of creation. Other inscriptions refer to Isis as the Great Goddess, who turns the earth in her orb, gives light to the sun, and to whom the stars are responsive.

To understand the exaltation expressed in these ancient Egyptian hymns, we have to first examine the cosmology that emerged in Heliopolis, the religious center dedicated to the worship of the sun god Re in the early dynastic period (c. 3000 BCE). According to the metaphysics of Heliopolis, the world emerged into light from the dark primordial waters when the god Atum, whose name means totality or void, manifested as a fertile hillock of mud. Atum, the dual creator who in his/her essence contained all that was yet to come into manifestation, generated the male Shu (air, space, light), and the female Tefnut (moisture, order). By exhaling these cosmic elements, Atum endowed everything with life force. Shu and Tefnut in turn brought forth the god Geb, the earth, and the goddess Nut, the sky. The sky goddess Nut is often depicted as arched over her consort, the earth god Geb, whose raised arms supported her so she could give birth to the stars after they sailed across her watery

---

[6] Quoted from Stone, *When God was a Woman*, Introduction

body believed to constitute the vault of heaven. Nut and Geb eventually gave birth to two additional pairs of gods and goddesses: Isis and Osiris, Seth and Nephthys, who represent the fourth generation of deities emerging from the formless primeval waters. The perception of Isis as the generative primordial matrix, as expressed in the quoted hymn from Thebes, derived from the function of the sky goddess Nut, mother of the sun, moon, and the stars. In Egyptian cosmology, Isis over time eventually came to be equated with Nut in whose body the great drama of the sun's creation – birth, growth, and death – was re—enacted each day and night.

Today we take for granted that the sun will rise, but in ancient Egypt the sun's rising was joyful and momentous. The visible sun was believed to emerge from the invisible and mysterious ground of being that harbored an infinite generative potential. In many of her representations, Isis – who was also worshipped as the "Maker of the Sunrise" and "Lightgiver to the Sun" because she helped to facilitate its emergence at dawn according to Egyptian cosmology – was depicted in the human form of a woman with headdress or crown that consisted of a solar disk centered between a pair of horns. Cow horns and cow ears were symbols that were also attributed to a goddess who likely predated Isis but later merged with her: Hathor. In *The Myth of the Goddess: Evolution of an Image*, Baring and Cashford tell us that the figure of Isis, who evolved over a period of thousands of years, did "merge in and out of other goddesses, as though the feminine principle were so all pervasive, its absence so inconceivable, that it could come into manifestation at any point as any character under any name."[7]

---

[7] Baring and Cashford, *The Myth of the Goddess*, p. 252.

Why does Isis, in addition to the solar disk, wear a crown of cow horns on her head? And how does this imagery symbolically relate to Egyptian cosmology? The vault of heaven was basically imagined as a great flood. This primeval watery abyss manifested at times in the form of a great cow nurturing the world with her rain—milk. This is an image that likely originated in the Neolithic period. The same conception is, not surprisingly, also reflected in the iconography that represents the sky goddess Nut as a cow believed to continuously give birth and provide milk, that is, sustaining the life she has brought forth from herself. Because of the perpetual generative function of the feminine, the great "sky cow," whose four legs represent the four cardinal points of the universe, eventually became a symbol of immortality. In honor of the great Cosmic Mother, sacred cows were kept in her temples and offerings were made to her. Especially women prayed to the cow—goddess for assistance in childbirth and for the power to conceive.

To truly understand the meaning of the milk giving "sky cow," it is important to note that ancient Egyptians attached substantial value to the cow, and viewed cows as a symbol of prosperity and abundance. Appreciating cows was a way to demonstrate pride in their thriving agricultural civilization. When Isis was depicted with horns, she was likely understood as an embodiment of the creative and vital life force that also expressed itself in and through the goddesses Nut and Hathor. A painted ceiling relief from the Hathor temple in Dendera shows the sky goddess Nut swallowing and giving birth to the sun god Ra, whose rays fall on the face of the goddess Hathor, who becomes the horizon that reflects the first rays of the morning sun. Not surprisingly, Hathor – and Isis for that matter – became identified with the fiery eye of Ra. The eye of the sun god Ra may also be looked at as a metaphor for in—sight, or inner vision, which is an essential and integral part of Egyptian metaphysics.

Ancient Egyptians believed that names or words originated from the primeval utterance of Atum, the creator. One story tells us how Isis obtained from Ra the secret of his name, and thus gained supremacy over him in knowing this "word of power." Similar to John's famous statement "In the Beginning was the Word/ Logos" and Kabbalist notions based on the function of Hebrew letters in the creation process, names were regarded as a blueprint, some sort of DNA that contained the divine characteristics of individuals such as, for example, their unique traits and skills. According to Egyptian metaphysics, the recipient of the knowledge of one's secret name was hence believed to gain complete power over the revealer. This aspect of Egyptian metaphysics is likely related to notions that later emerged in the Jewish tradition, emphasizing that the sacred name of YHVH, the "Most Holy One," may not be uttered.

The narrative of how Isis obtained from Ra the power of his secret name gave rise to the conception of Isis being "a wiser magician than any other god," as she is referred to in the aforementioned hymn from Thebes. Egyptians perceived her as a source of profound esoteric wisdom and magic power. In the Egyptian worldview, wisdom came from insight into the mystery of life and death that was ever—present in the steady rhythm of the agricultural cycle and the annual flooding of the Nile.

Wall painting of Isis, ca. 1360 BCE

Isis as the Great Mother and Facilitator of Civilization

Egypt's agricultural economy and efficient trading
network extended to Lebanon, Mesopotamia, and Punt in
eastern Africa (likely modern—day Somalia and Ethiopia),
and was largely supported by the Nile River. The Greek
historian Herodotus, who lived in the fifth century BCE,
proclaimed Egypt to be the "gift of the Nile," a statement
that emphasized the tremendous significance of the Nile
within Egyptian civilization. The rising and receding of
the waters of this mighty river demonstrated the annual
cycle of death and rebirth so essential to the Egyptian
worldview. In mid—June, around the time of the summer
solstice, the Nile seemed to disappear, shrunk to half its
size. Yet just when life reached its lowest ebb, and the
fields, cattle and people became thirsty and dry, the Nile
began to swell again, slowly at first but gathering force
until the tumbling waters burst forth and spilled over
miles of flat and shriveled land on each side of the river.
From July to October, all things appeared to regress into
the primordial state of watery chaos from which all life

97

had emerged, and from which life would eventually come forth once again. In autumn, the waters dropped, the inundation receded, and the fields were fertilized by the rich layers of muck left from their annual inundation, and were pregnant with life and ready for seeding in November.

Beyond the dark and fertile soil lay the arid and rocky desert burnt bare by the sun, an area in which nothing grew. These sands were always moving toward the wetlands, ready to encroach on the cultivated fields. The contrast between life and death was hence ever—present; and the perception of water as the origin of life, mirrored in the rhythmic flow and ebb of the Nile, became a common feature of Egyptian creation mythology.

In some mythic narratives, the goddess Isis is referred to as the "Creatress of the Nile Flood" because ancient Egyptians identified her with the star Sothis (also called Sirius) that appeared when the rising of the water was imminent. Yet Egyptians were not only skilled observers of the motion of stars. They also began to experiment with agriculture, likely before 5000 BCE, and it is safe to conclude that this provided a relatively stable and regular supply of food during the Neolithic period. Indeed, agriculture soon generated a surplus in Egypt. This meant that for the first time human beings were able to produce more food than they needed for survival. Eventually, the agricultural surplus also led to a dramatic increase of the human population and to the concentration of large numbers of people in villages and cities. Another consequence of this surplus was that labor became more specialized. Over time this led to sharp social distinctions based on accumulated wealth. Certain individuals were now free to concentrate their talents on enterprises other than the cultivation of the fields and food production. In this context, Isis' contributions to Egyptian civilization were viewed as being remarkable. It was believed that Isis was knowledgeable about the natural processes of gestation and regeneration, and that she assisted pregnant women in delivery and instructed her people in the skills of crossbreeding of plants and the domestication and breeding of animals. She also trained them to master some of the earliest crafts such as weaving, pottery, corn grinding, and bread baking. In gratitude, the people offered her ears of corn, the first fruits of the harvest. Isis was also concerned with family issues and the establishment of marriage as an institution. In contrast to Inanna, maternal devotion was central to the nature of Isis. In some of her most enduring images, she is represented as a mother seated on a lion throne, holding her infant—son Horus lovingly in her lap.

Representations of Isis as the "Great Mother" embracing and suckling her son—god Horus clearly inspired the widely popular mother—child— iconography of Mother Mary holding the child Jesus that emerged in the Christian tradition many centuries later. Praised as the "eternal savior of the human race" who bestows a mother's tender affections on the misfortunes of distressed mortal humans, ancient Egyptians prayed to Isis for cures and healings from numerous diseases. Isis was said to possess the magic healing skills necessary to cure infants bitten by venomous snakes and scorpions.

On pectorals and in tombs, Isis appears often as the winged goddess, spreading her arm—wings over her people as the great protective Mother. The winged Isis serves as a representation reminiscent of Neolithic bird goddesses.

The Goddess in her function as a cultural heroine and facilitator of civilization can also be found in Native American belief. Several North American tribes venerate White Buffalo Calf Woman as a wise woman and teacher who introduced them to the sacred medicine pipe and the seven sacred ceremonies, one of which is the Sun Dance.

Conceptions of Women in Isis' Egypt

Did veneration of Isis as the "Great Mother" affect how Egyptians viewed their own human mothers? Did this translate into Egyptian women having a status equivalent to that of men? What role did women play in ancient Egypt and what was their overall situation? Generally speaking, the texts and sepulchral monuments show that mothers and wives enjoyed a high position and were treated with respect. As a rule, a man had only one legal wife, though he may have possessed several concubines. The relationship between husband and wife is often described as cordial and intimate. On funerary monuments they stand or sit side by side, the wife folding her arms around her husband, and she is present when he goes hunting or fishing. Until the end of the Middle Kingdom (c. 1786 BCE), women were equal with men before the law. Not only could they inherit property, they could also dispose of it as they saw fit. Historians refer to this type of society, in which bloodlines are traced through the female and property is inherited through female lineage, as matrilineal. If there were no male heirs in a ruling family, a woman could even inherit the throne, as happened more than once. Queen Hatshepsut (1503—1482 BCE), for example, was one of the most prominent female pharaohs. In addition to being able to inherit the throne, women also participated in religious functions and held other prestigious positions. They served as priestesses, healers, magicians, and even scribes.

Symbolic Aspects of the Goddess Isis

In the aforementioned hymn from Thebes dating from the fourteenth century BCE, Isis is called "Mistress of the two Lands of Egypt." This title refers to the time when Upper and Lower Egypt were unified by the legendary King Menes, which happened roughly around 3000 BCE. According to tradition, Menes founded the city of Memphis, which stood at the junction of Upper and Lower Egypt. The two lands of Egypt attributed to Isis in this hymn from Thebes were symbolically represented by two goddesses. It appears likely that both goddesses originated from Neolithic bird and snake goddesses. The goddess of Lower Egypt assumed the form of a serpent, Wadjet of the Delta. The goddess of Upper Egypt appeared as a vulture, the goddess Nekhbet. This makes perfect sense when considering the geography of the region. Cobras were frequently found curled up beside their eggs amid the tall papyrus grasses of the Delta swamps, while vultures hovered over the arid desert plateau of Upper Egypt. The vulture and the serpent, displayed on Isis' headdress, commonly framed the entrances to temples. While vulture and serpent were viewed as symbolizing the union of the two lands on the external level, they also represented, on a more esoteric—mystical level, the union beyond all duality that arises in awakened states of consciousness.

The Egyptian vulture goddess Nekhbet may have been related to the great Goddess of Death and Regeneration in Neolithic art. Sometimes Nekhbet was also pictured as a serpent. The serpent goddess, Wadjet, appeared as the royal *uraeus*, the rearing and spitting cobra centered on the foreheads of deities and pharaohs known as the fiery "Eye of Ra," the sun god. Jules Cashford and Anne Baring describe the ancient association of goddess and serpent as so close that one of the hieroglyphs for goddess was, indeed, a serpent. A painting from the tomb of Seti I (c. 1300 BCE) in the famous Valley of the Kings in Thebes shows Isis and her sister Nephthys as serpent goddesses carrying the crowns of Lower and Upper Egypt. Wadjet was commonly affiliated with Isis in her form as serpent and also in her function as the "Eye of Ra" symbolizing illumination and wisdom.

In addition to the serpent, Isis was associated with an image of a high—backed throne that rested upon her head and served, at the same time, as the hieroglyph of her name. The throne recalls the primeval order, for in its form lies the original mound, the "High Hill," which first emerged from the waters as habitable land. The hill represented the goddess as matter/form/earth across the cultures. In an extension of this symbolism, the lap of Isis literally and symbolically became the royal throne of Egypt. In numerous representations, the pharaoh is enthroned on her lap, the seat of power, as her "son—lover." To be nursed from her breast was to receive divine sustenance and guidance that would legitimize the pharaoh's rule and endow him with the skills of kingship. Not surprisingly, pharaohs came to view themselves as "sons of Isis," the Great Mother. Eventually, the kings were regarded as fully divine embodiments of the god Horus, the falcon—headed son of Isis. In her role as the mother of the pharaoh, who ruled the unified land as her son in her place, Isis ultimately became an expression of the cosmic order and how it was mirrored by the societal structure of Egyptian civilization.

In some of her representations, Isis displays the ostrich feather of the double crown of Upper and Lower Egypt on her head. The ostrich feather was a symbol of Maat, the goddess through whom the fundamental laws of the universe were manifested. Maat was viewed as an embodiment of eternal truth, impeccable justice, and perfect balance. She represented the cosmic order that had emerged from primordial chaos. This order found its expression primarily in the fundamental moral—ethical tenets of ancient Egypt. People were expected to live "by Maat, in Maat, and for Maat." In her function as the goddess who binds the human world to the realm of the deities within the one universal law, Maat may be comparable in principle to the *tao* in Chinese philosophy, the *dharma* in India, or Sophia in the Wisdom literature of the Judeo—Christian scriptures.

Seated on Isis' throne, the pharaoh would hold a tiny figure of the goddess Maat in his hand as a symbol that he represented the divine order. Isis is the "kingmaker," similar to Inanna in Mesopotamia. Men ruled as kings in these ancient Near Eastern civilizations, but it was the power of these goddesses that enabled and endorsed their rule.

The Mysteries of Isis and Osiris

The Greek author Plutarch (c. 40—120 CE), upon whose version the following account is based, was the first to provide a complete narrative of the mythical drama of Isis and Osiris. According to Plutarch, Isis ruled in Egypt with her brother—husband Osiris, whose generative powers enabled the land watered by the Nile to be fertile and productive. As the oldest son of Geb and Nut, Osiris inherited the right to govern Egypt, and he was known as the giver of the seeds, the "plant of life." Isis was believed to have instructed her people with the skills of plant crossbreeding, and together these deities contributed to an abundant harvest. As representatives of the domain of swamps, rivers, and mud, both Isis and Osiris experienced the mysteries of insemination in the earth's womb and the gestation of new life in the depths of darkness.

Osiris was believed to have taught the people of Egypt to raise crops, build cities and irrigation canals, worship the deities, and devise a legal system. During his absence, Osiris left the government of the kingdom to Isis, who ruled vigilantly and wisely on his behalf. However, Osiris' brother Seth soon came to be depicted as the great opponent, who sought to kill Osiris and claim the sovereignty of the kingdom for himself.

The people of Egypt believed that Isis and Osiris had loved each other ever since their time together in the womb of their mother, the sky goddess, Nut. Isis' unification with Osiris in Nut's womb may also be looked at, from a more esoteric perspective, as a metaphor of the harmonious existence of both feminine and masculine qualities in Isis' psyche. Because the cult of Isis was to a great extent rooted in the mythology that arose around the death and resurrection of her beloved spouse, the myth of Osiris' kingship and subsequent demise may be briefly summarized.

Seth, the brother of Isis and Osiris, became envious of Osiris' power and success as a king. Moreover, he fell passionately in love with Isis. To satisfy his malevolent desires, he decided to usurp the throne and take Isis as his wife. As the obstructive power in ancient Egypt, Seth was commonly affiliated with chaotic forces, destruction, death, drought, and the desert. As the representative of the evil universal principle, he embodied an archetypal figure encountered across the cultures. As the destroyer of the status quo, he acted as a cosmic force, a catalyst that would challenge the integrity and the wisdom of Isis and Osiris. Seth secretly ascertained his brother's measurements and promptly had a casket fashioned to fit Osiris' size. During a banquet in honor of Osiris, Seth informed his guests that the casket would be awarded to the individual whose body would be a perfect match. He persuaded Osiris to get into the casket to test its size. As soon as Osiris followed through, Seth's assistants quickly closed the coffin and set it afloat on the Nile.

Upon hearing of this heinous act, Isis uttered lamentations that were heard throughout the land. In ancient times wailing women took part in the funerary processions that accompanied the deceased to their grave in Egypt. Most likely, this Egyptian mortuary practice had its roots in this mythology on which the cult of Isis and Osiris was based. These lamentations, however, were not just an expression of grief. They also served as invocations believed to possess magical power. Isis' lamentations were hence also meant to call Osiris back to life. Isis didn't just engage in lamentations – she decided to take a more proactive role by embarking on a quest for her husband's casket. Her extensive wanderings can be read as both an external and internal journey. They may be looked upon as an effort on Isis' part to reclaim her truth and her spiritual center that had been wounded with Osiris' demise. With the perseverance and the patience so characteristic of her, Isis learned that the coffin had been washed ashore at Byblos in Phoenicia (modern—day Lebanon) and that it was to be found inside the trunk of a tamarisk tree. Because of Osiris' great fertilizing powers, the tree's bark had grown, eventually encapsulating the entire coffin. In this context, it may be helpful to look at the broader symbolic significance of the tree in ancient Egypt.

Trees were scarce in Egypt, and most had to be imported from Lebanon. Partly as a result, trees were considered to be sacred, especially the sycamore and the acacia which were thought of as symbols of eternal life and renewal. Isis is sometimes depicted on tomb walls as growing from a tree trunk, and leaning forward to provide the deceased with food and drink. Over time, the tree became a symbol of the central nervous system and the spine, particularly the sacrum of Osiris (the sacrum is a large triangular bone at the base of the spine.). Perhaps ancient Egyptians believed in a chakra system similar to Indian Kundalini Yoga, in which life energy – conceived of as a metaphysical coiled serpent – rises up from the base of the spine, as noted. The tree, sometimes referred to as the *djed* pillar, was considered to be a symbol of stability and durability reminiscent of the Tree of Life, the 'world axis,' the universal tree that plays a significant role in many traditions. Osiris, caught in tree and time, is comparable to other major savior figures across the cultures. Examples are the Buddha meditating under the bodhi tree, Jesus on the Tree of Life as a variation of the Christian cross, and Odin's nine days of suffering on the world tree, Yggdrasil, during which he acquired the wisdom of the runes, the Nordic alphabet. A similar symbolism applies also to Osiris, who is caught in the tree coffin, the world axis that constitutes the center of reality from which new creation emerges.

The tree grown around Osiris' coffin was, in fact, so majestic that the local rulers had it felled and fashioned into a pillar for their palace. Isis succeeded in obtaining

the coffin—pillar and brought it back to Egypt. As soon
as she was alone with the coffin, she opened it, laid her
face on her dead husband, and wept in a heartbreaking
way. Isis' lamentations, meant to bring Osiris back to life,
restored his *ka*, an extremely complex power in Egyptian
metaphysics that may be defined as the vital force or
generative essence that informs the more subtle bodies.
At this point, Isis initiates a major act of procreation. This
act is commonly depicted by showing Isis in the form of
a bird descending upon the revived phallus of Osiris with
the purpose of impregnating herself with his seed. Horus,
the falcon—headed child conceived from this union,
has to grow up in a hidden location to be protected from
Seth's destructive machinations. Isis also makes sure to
hide the coffin enclosing the body of Osiris in the remote
marshes of the Nile delta.

Unfortunately, Seth finds the coffin hidden among the
reeds during her absence. He cuts the body of Osiris into
fourteen pieces, each of which he scatters across Egypt.
The bodily dismemberment may be viewed as a metaphor
for the psycho—spiritual fragmentation of the archetypal
power that Osiris embodied as the god—king of fertility.
When Isis learned of the dismemberment of her husband,
she filled the countryside with her cries and embarked
for the second time on a long and arduous journey in
search of his body parts. With help from other deities, Isis
retrieved all the parts with the exception of the phallus
that had been swallowed by a fish. Interestingly, the
fish had been a symbol of generative powers since the
pre—dynastic period in Egypt. Wherever Isis finds a piece
of Osiris' body, she buries it, performs the appropriate
rites, and she has a temple or shrine erected in his honor.
Moreover, the Pyramid Texts tell us that Isis flaps her
wings, hereby providing Osiris with the breath of life. Her
wisdom and magical potency, assisting most prominently

in the healing of people who have been bitten by venomous snakes and stung by scorpions, plays a pivotal role in the process of restoring life to her husband.

According to Plutarch's version of the mythic narrative, ancient Egyptians believed that Osiris was resurrected after his dismemberment. Whether he returned to life as a spirit or in physical form remains elusive, although we are told that he retained the power of speech and thought. After his miraculous resurrection, he became the lord of the *Duat*, the underworld. For thousands of years, Egyptians thrived on the notion of the god—man's immortality. This belief was expressed in imagery that equated Osiris with the new cycle of vegetative growth. He is pictured as a mummy with grain sprouting from his body while a priest pours water over him. As king of the deceased, Osiris presided over the hall of judgment where each individual's heart was weighed to determine whether the person was worthy of being granted immortality. Indeed, it was this sublime concept of an afterlife in Duat that endowed the ancient Egyptians with strength, optimism, perseverance, and, most importantly, with the enduring hope that they too would eventually partake in this most desirable of all gifts, namely, eternal existence. From the earliest dynasties to the end of the New Kingdom (c. 1075 BCE), the *Mysteries of Osiris and Isis* – enacted secretly in temple sanctuaries – celebrated Osiris' resurrection in which the entire universe participated.

Isis' significance grew significantly over time. Her cult was originally centered in Philae, at the southern border of Egypt, but the cult later expanded to other parts of the kingdom. During the Hellenistic period (after 320 BCE), she acquired great popularity in the countries around the Mediterranean basin and was sometimes identified with goddesses such as the Greek Grain Mother, Demeter, or Cybele, the Great Mother of Anatolia (modern—day Turkey). Isis gradually assumed universal importance, a fact that is reflected in one of her numerous titles: "Savior of the Human Race." Because of her unwavering courage and her capability to redeem herself after the demise of her husband, Isis served as an inspirational and comforting example to her devotees in distress. The cult of Isis – open to both women and men – took the form of a mystery religion that, later, rapidly spread across the Roman Empire. This may also have been a result of a widespread spiritual malaise. The popular masses found great solace in cults and sacred rites that provided a sense of purpose, and promised salvation and eternal life. In his book *The Golden Ass*, the Roman philosopher Apuleius, who wrote in the second century CE and was an initiate of the *Mysteries of Isis*, provides an account of the rite through which her followers gained insight into the depths of esoteric wisdom. The culmination appears to have been the *epopteia*, a vision of the highest truth that may have occurred as a result of dramatizing representations of the narrative upon which the mysteries were founded. Initiates voluntarily died to their "old selves" – or what we may also refer to as ego—death – and experienced subsequent rebirth into more evolved and awakened stages and states of consciousness. Eventually, initiates hoped to attain the gift of immortality bestowed upon them by Isis, the compassionate Mother.

Isis fulfilled a variety of functions in ancient Egypt. She acted as the proactive and compassionate wife who restored her husband to life by her perseverance and her healing skills. As the Great Mother of life, death, and regeneration, she suffered trial and loss just like any ordinary human being. Her display of grief and her vulnerability to life's vicissitudes – one aspect of her personality – may also explain her enduring appeal as a goddess who lives out the archetypal drama of every woman and man. Of all Egyptian goddesses, only Isis, who dwelled among humans, possesses an individual character and a personalized story. As a sister, wife, and mother who engages in authentic love and sacred sexual relations, she adds a new dimension to the image of the Universal Mother. The mythic narrative of Isis reflects a metaphysics that does not perceive logos/spirit and matter/flesh as being separate and antagonistic to each other, as is the case in most of the subsequent religious traditions.

While Isis was primarily worshipped for her protective, healing, nurturing, and compassionate qualities, she also served as a role model of strength, reason, and autonomy. Neither passive, nor succumbing to the suffering she endured, she remained empowered and faced her challenges. Isis was in touch with the deepest dimensions of both her divinity and her embodied human nature. By connecting with the deepest core of her being, she was able to reconcile herself with the trials inherent in the human condition while also transcending her suffering and the limitations of her embodiment. She used neither military might nor brute force, but relied instead on her own magical powers. As an adept in exerting these powers, Isis served as a source of profound esoteric wisdom and insight into the mysteries of life and death. Once reunited with her husband, she assisted him in Duat, providing the living with hope and the deceased with sustenance. Independent, self—reliant, and sensitive to her own needs as well as to those of others, her multidimensional personality may be regarded as the prototype of a fully integrated goddess—woman, who is an embodiment of spirit and flesh, logos and compassion.

MINOAN CRETE – THE FLOWERING OF GODDESS CULTURE

Minoan Civilization and Culture

"Out in the dark blue sea there lies a land called Crete, a rich and lovely land, washed by the waves on every side..."[8] These words in Homer's *Odyssey* evoke a visionary island, an almost dreamlike Eden in the Mediterranean basin where many of the Greek goddesses and gods were said to have been born. Homer, the legendary Greek poet, who likely wrote in the eighth century BCE, was once the only source for these fabulous beginnings, so we couldn't be certain that his poetic vision was historically accurate.

This changed in the first quarter of the twentieth century when the British archaeologist Sir Arthur Evans learned more about this mysterious island civilization which dated back to the Neolithic era, at which time a small colony of immigrants, probably from Anatolia, first arrived on the island's shores. By the late third millennium BCE a technologically advanced and socially complex culture arose in Crete. Scholars refer to this sophisticated and elegant culture – the first great civilization of Europe – as Minoan, named after its legendary king Minos. Between 2200 BCE and 1700 BCE, the inhabitants of Crete built a series of lavish palaces throughout the island, most notably the enormous complex at Knossos.

---

[8] Homer, Odyssey, 19.

These palaces had perfect drainage systems and convenient sanitary installations. The vivid frescoes found in Knossos and in other Minoan palaces display remarkable sensitivity and a delight in beauty, grace, and movement.

An exuberant joy in all that was alive found artistic expression in scenes depicting natural motifs such as lilies, birds, butterflies, and dolphins. The artists captured fleeting moments such as the arching up of a dolphin, flight of a bird, and leaping of a bull. Other motifs typically encountered in Minoan art include ceremonies and rituals that display harmony between men and women who joyfully intermingle as equal partners and participants in life. A prominent female figurine – commonly referred to as Goddess or "queen—priestess" by scholars – makes her ubiquitous appearance on golden seals, pottery, palace frescos, and in numerous elaborate faience statuettes. On seals, she rests in the shape of a bee, or stands upon a mountain flanked by lions. Some of the seals depict her sitting beneath the Tree of Life, offering the fruits of the earth to her priestesses and her devotees.

The Minoan palaces fulfilled political, economic, and religious functions. They contained multiple stories, at different heights, that were asymmetrically arranged around vast courtyards, majestic facades, and hundreds of rooms. This asymmetrical room and apartment arrangement – reminiscent of the labyrinth in its architectural structure – was yet another unique feature of Minoan culture that may have inspired later Greek myths recounting the existence of an impenetrable labyrinth situated beneath the palace of Knossos. Some of the palace rooms served as storage places used for the orderly safekeeping of food reserves and all sorts of treasures. The island's economy was originally agrarian; but as time passed, stock breeding, elaborate crafts such as pottery and fine jewelry, and, most importantly, trade assumed increasing importance, greatly contributing to the economic prosperity of the island. Between 2200 and 1450 BCE, Crete was a major hub of Mediterranean commerce. By 2200 BCE, due to its geographical location in the east—central Mediterranean, Minoan ships sailed to Greece, Anatolia, Phoenicia, and Egypt, where they exchanged Cretan wine, olive oil, and wool for grains, textiles, and manufactured goods. The recording of trading products and food supply was facilitated by the Minoan palace officials' two writing systems, which had both come into use by c. 1700 BCE. The first included a series of pictorial symbols termed Minoan hieroglyphs. The second script, known as Linear A, consisted of signs written in straight lines as opposed to the pictorial symbols. Unfortunately, linguists have not been able to decipher Linear A, the most prominent of the script types displayed on Cretan clay tablets.

A Peace—Loving Culture and Society

In addition to the numerous storage rooms, the palace complexes contained rooms used for ceremonial worship, although Minoans generally favored open—air sanctuaries on the top of mountains and in sacred caves for their rituals. Two thrones were found at the palace of Knossos, one of which was located in a public audience chamber in the residential quarters, and is, today, the oldest seat of royal authority found in Europe. These thrones suggest that some form of centralized governmental administration must have existed; yet centralization doesn't necessarily imply autocratic rule and exploitation, even though oppressive political systems were already the norm in practically all of the other major Bronze Age civilizations. Although social distinctions and an affluent ruling class likely existed in Crete, there is no archaeological indication that their power was backed up by massive armed force. Nor does evidence exist that the numerous city—states within the island – Knossos, Mallia, Phaistos, Zakros, and Hagia Triada being the most prominent ones – fought (as was the norm in ancient Sumer).

The lack of an armed intervention force to support the ruling establishment was eventually related to another of the many remarkable features of Cretan society, namely, an equitable sharing of wealth. Again, this was in sharp contrast to other major civilization at that time. The archaeological evidence for a more egalitarian distribution of wealth in Minoan society lies in the fact that none of the homes excavated so far indicate poor living conditions. Moreover, all the Cretan towns and palaces lack military fortifications – another striking contrast to the walled cities of other major Bronze Age civilizations. The absence of precautionary defensive systems was likely due to the fact that in general Minoans felt relatively safe from armed threats and potential invasions because they lived on an island. Not surprisingly, idealized scenes of warfare and brutal oppression of captives are thus absent in the artistic tradition of the Minoans, who are commonly characterized as a peace—loving people by scholars.

What Led to the Decline of Minoan Culture?

The decline of this exceptionally sophisticated island culture is controversial. Two factors stand out: natural catastrophes and foreign domination. It appears that in the centuries after 1700 BCE Minoan society experienced a series of destructive earthquakes, tidal waves, and volcanic eruptions on the island of Thera north of

Crete. After each of these calamities, the people of Crete embarked on a new round of palace—building to replace the destroyed multistoried structures. Also, although Crete escaped the threat of invasion for many centuries, this changed during the late palatial period. After 1450 BCE, the wealth of Minoan society attracted a series of invaders from the sea, despite the relative safety of Crete's geographical location. Across the entire island, archaeological excavations have revealed signs of burning and destruction – as if the area had been ransacked by invaders. By 1100 BCE, Crete had fallen under the domination of an Indo—European people – named the Mycenaean culture after one of their most prominent settlements – who had expanded their influence beyond peninsular Greece. Yet Minoan culture and traditions would continue to deeply influence the inhabitants of nearby mainland Greece for centuries.

Minoan Ceremonial Worship

The religion of Minoan civilization centered on a joyful celebration of nature. Minoan religious rituals were far more intimately involved with natural life than were the rites of other Bronze Age civilizations such as ancient Egypt and Babylonia. Minoan ceremonial worship usually took place at sacred sites on mountain tops, in cave sanctuaries, and in meadows in the vicinity of groves and springs where rustic shrines and altars had been erected. The sacred caves typically possessed subterranean chambers connected through passages and wells of pure water. Because of their particular shape, their impenetrable darkness, and their damp walls, caves were clearly related to the "womb and tomb" symbolism. Evidence exists that several Cretan caves were affiliated with the function of giving birth. Exploration of Minoan cave sanctuaries has brought to light numerous religious artifacts such as altars, vessels, figurines, and objects that clearly reflect regenerative themes and motifs. Similar to the caves, which served as dramatic and powerful religious sanctuaries, mountain peaks also evoked a profound sense of the sacred. Many legendary deities were believed to live on mountaintops. Archaeologists have discovered numerous impressive sanctuaries and altar offerings on Cretan mountain peaks, such as, for example, on Mount Juktas, one of the most sacred mountains on the island. The notched peak of this mountain can be seen directly to the south from the palace sanctuary of Knossos. Similar to other cultures, Minoans came to view mountains eventually as cosmic pillars that united heaven and earth. Throughout the most splendid periods of their civilization, the people of ancient Crete went to great lengths to perform their rites on steep and almost inaccessible mountain slopes where they could best connect with their Goddess.

Snake Goddess of Knossos

Manifestations and Symbols of the Minoan Goddess

What are the manifestations, symbols, and functions of this Minoan Goddess? Some of the most intriguing objects recovered from the palace treasures of Knossos represent her as a "Snake Goddess." Most of these refined and elegant faience statuettes dating from c. 1600 BCE are about thirteen inches tall, and their eyes display a trance—like gaze. One of these goddesses wears a crisscrossed patterned skirt reminiscent of Neolithic art. The net patterned skirt suggests that she is the weaver of the web of life, which is continuously re—created from the amniotic fluid of her womb. Her skirt exhibits seven flounced layers, which may have been a reference to the number of days of the moon's four quarters that divide into two the waxing and waning halves of the lunar cycle. A tight bodice exposes her breasts, which offer the gift of nurture. In each hand, she is holding up a snake with the ritualized gesture of a powerful sacred statement. This figurine may have been a representation of the Goddess, her priestess performing snake dances, or another ritual related to the new regenerative cycle after the winter season. The two snakes held up by the Goddess may have symbolized duality – life and death, time and eternity – which is ultimately reconciled by the Goddess who represents unity beyond the polar opposites.

In addition to the snakes in the palms of her hands, the goddess also displays a tame lion cub resting on her head. Lions frequently appear as guardians of the Goddess on Minoan seals. In Crete, both wild and tamed animals were considered sacred. In her manifestations as the "Goddess of the Animals," she is sometimes also referred to as "Lady of the Beasts." The Goddess of the Animals appears not only in Minoan art, but is a ubiquitous figure in ancient Sumer, Egypt, and Anatolia. In classical

Greece, she reemerged most as Artemis, goddess of the raw and untamed natural forces, commonly portrayed accompanied by wild animals such as, for example, a stag or a doe.

In another version, the bare—breasted "Snake Goddess" holds the head of a snake in her right hand and its tail in her left hand; the serpent's body is wrapped around her shoulders and back. Two additional snakes entwine themselves around her waist and coil up her arms. A serpent spirals around her headdress, similar to the *uraeus* serpent adorning Egyptian deities and pharaohs. Two intertwined snakes on her belly may refer to the goddess' power of birthing new life and, at the same time, may refer to her power to take life back into the seamless unity that is the ground of being. Snakes, a common motif in Minoan art, can be found coiled around pots, urns, and vases. At times, the snake goddess also takes the form of a vessel designed to pour libations, most commonly milk or blood, over shrines and altars.

Controversy exists regarding whether the Snake Goddess statuettes represent the Minoan goddess, her priestess, or a queen—priestess who may have occupied the throne. The frescoes of the aforementioned throne room in the palace of Knossos exhibit ornamental griffins guarding the throne. In *The Myth of the Goddess: Evolution of an Image*, Anne Baring and Jules Cashford remind us that the griffin, a mythical being that is a composite image of bird, lion, and snake, embodies the three dimensions of sky, earth, and underground water sources that characterized the three aspects of the great Goddess of the Neolithic period. To this point, no representations of a male king or a dominant male figure whatsoever have been found in Crete. In the palace frescoes, male figures are always young men, and often they are represented as smaller in size than the prominent female who is commonly interpreted to be the Goddess or the high priestess who represented her. In most cases, these young men assume the posture of supplicants. In one fresco from the palace—shrine at Knossos dating from the fifteenth century BCE, two converging lines of young men attend the Goddess who is the central figure. Some of the males raise their arms in homage, others carry wine offerings in large vessels called rhytons. The Goddess or her priestess is a lovely woman, fashionably dressed and coiffed. She wears a tight bodice that reveals her full breasts. Her dark hair is carefully arranged in long ringlets that frame her face. Both female and male figures exult in their physicality with erect posture, proud movements, and graceful gestures. In addition to the aforementioned absence of all scenes of idealized warfare in Minoan art, the fact that no dominant male figure exists fuels speculation that Crete might have been ruled by a "queen—priestess." Although it is tempting to believe this, the historical evidence for this argument remains inconclusive.

Did these Snake Goddesses represent the Minoan Goddess or just her priestess? Although the Goddess was often identified with the high priestess believed to be her earthly representation, the presence of numerous snakes suggests that the figurines are indeed goddesses in this particular case, as Anne Baring and Jules Cashford allege. The bare—breasted Goddess is also portrayed on sealstones displaying waterbirds instead of snakes. Miniature shrines from Knossos representing the Goddess exhibit doves resting on sacred pillars. In small votive figures found at household shrines, the Goddess has doves adorning her headdress. This symbolic bird is frequently affiliated with the Goddess in Minoan art, and its clay representations have been found in numerous cave sanctuaries, which may suggest that the doves served as votive offerings. According to Marija Gimbutas, an unbroken continuity exists between Neolithic bird and snake goddesses and Minoan civilization. Interestingly, the dove reappears centuries later in classical Greek mythology as the symbolic bird of the goddess of love and beauty, Aphrodite. The dove eventually came to symbolize sexual passion and the soul's return to the Goddess after death. The Romans called her Venus Columba, Venus—in—the—Dove. Her catacombs, mausoleums, and necropolis were known as *columbaria*, dovecotes. Later yet, the dove was adopted as a symbol of the Holy Spirit in Christianity. Originally however, the bird represented Sophia, God's feminine aspect affiliated with wisdom in the Jewish tradition and in early Christianity.

Another sealstone dating from c.1500 BCE shows the Goddess standing on a mountain peak, holding a scepter in one of her hands. She is flanked by two guardian lions. Symbolically, the lion is also related to the griffin, a composite image of lion, bird, and snake as depicted on the frescoes of the so—called throne room in the palace of Knossos.

Another epiphany of the Minoan Goddess was the bee, a symbol of regeneration with Neolithic roots. The Goddess in the shape of a bee appears on Minoan seals since the late third millennium BCE. Baring and Cashford have suggested that the humming of the bee may have been heard by the Minoans as the "voice" of the Goddess emulating the sound of creation. They remind us of an ancient belief stating that bees arise from the carcass of a sacrificial bull. In this renewal symbolism, bees are not only perceived as a resurrected version of the dead bull, but also as representing the souls of the deceased. Not surprisingly, honey was used to embalm and preserve the bodies of the dead.

Correspondences Between Minoan Religious Practices and the Greek Oracle at Delphi

The importance of bee keeping is documented in hieroglyphic drawings of beehives that were found in Crete, and may have inspired cultures that emerged later in Greece. The tombs in Mycenae, for example, were shaped as beehives, and the same applies to the *omphalos* stone, the "navel of the earth," at the famous Delphic oracle. Delphi, which is etymologically related to the word for womb, was viewed as the birthplace of the universe during the period of classical Greece. This major pilgrimage site was ruled by the god Apollo and by his chief oracular priestess Pythia, who was referred to as the Delphic bee. Honey also played an important role in Minoan rituals. It was fermented into mead and drunk as an intoxicating potion during ecstatic rites that were similar to rites celebrated in honor of the god Dionysus centuries later. At Ephesus, the Greek goddess Artemis was equally affiliated with the bee as her insect epiphany, and her priestesses were called *melissai*, which is the Greek word for bee.

Together with the bee, the butterfly was another important symbol of regeneration affiliated with numerous ancient goddesses. Across the cultures, the butterfly has commonly been viewed as an image of transformation and of the soul's journey. This becomes evident when we consider that the Greek words for butterfly and soul were identical: *psyche*. The butterfly is likely related symbolically to the ubiquitous *labrys*, the double ax in Minoan culture. Marija Gimbutas opines that the schematic butterflies on European Neolithic pots are the precursor to the later emerging Minoan double axes. The process of transformation from butterfly to double axe was likely influenced by the similarity of the shape, according to Gimbutas. The puzzling double ax appears in Minoan crypts, tombs, altars, and on numerous seals. This symbol most likely marked entrances and enclosures of sanctuaries. In certain cases, the Goddess and/or her priestesses are depicted holding the double axes in their hands while performing their sacred rites. Minoan seals dating back from c.1600 BCE even portray the Goddess with the wings of a butterfly stylized into the shape of a double ax. Gimbutas attaches significance to this symbol, saying that the double ax is likely the supreme emblem of the Goddess in her regenerative aspect. This symbol appears in anthropomorphic form with a human head on some occasions; in other examples the handle of the double ax appears in the form of a tree trunk or as emerging from the crescent shaped horns of a bull.

The Double Ax, Tree of Life, Bullhorn, and Other Minoan Religious Iconography

One of the numerous Minoan seals dating from c. 1500 BCE depicts the Goddess with the double ax seated beneath the Tree of Life. As in ancient Egypt and Mesopotamia, the tree – and its variant form the sacred pillar – may have signified the world axis. The same seal shows the Goddess offering her nurturing breasts to her devotees, welcoming two women, probably priestesses, with three poppies full of seeds. Poppies were regarded as a sacred plant of transformation also used for medicinal purposes. Some of the symbols displayed on this particular artifact are ubiquitous in Minoan art. For example, one of the most common representations of the great Goddess found in Cretan household shrines portray her in the form of a tubular shaped body as if emerging from a tree—pillar. Her upper torso resembles a female with arms raised in prayer. Her crown consists of poppies that will eventually induce a trance—like state. Poppies were grown in great quantities in Crete and likely used in sacred rituals to elicit visionary experiences. This Minoan seal may have displayed the joyful celebration of rebirth after death, as also suggested by the artist's choice of placing the vibrant sun next to the waning moon at the top of the same seal.

Double axes emerging from bullhorns are equally common in Minoan art. The sacred ax was the ritualistic instrument that was applied to sacrifice the bull, the cult animal who embodied regenerative powers. Baring and Cashford point out that the sacrifice of the bull, symbol of fertility and potency, was believed to renew the life cycle in a way that was similar to the ceremonial cutting down of the tree. Countless bull models were found in Cretan caves and tombs. In some cases, representations of bulls display vegetation sprouting from their bodies, similar to the plants growing from Osiris' body, who, coincidentally, was also known as the "bull god" in ancient Egypt. These examples provide ample evidence of the life force as symbolized by the bull. It appears likely that this symbolism has its roots in the Neolithic period. The Goddess giving birth to the bull as her son is a motif already encountered in Neolithic art. In Minoan culture, the bull could equally be referred to as the "son" of the Goddess, according to Baring and Cashford. In some cases the bull is revealed as the figure of a young man or young god. This male figure, diminutive in size in relation to the Goddess, is depicted on seal stones as either descending toward the Goddess or standing bent backwards in adoration before her in the posture of salutation. The symbolic affiliation between the bull and the young god—man in Minoan culture is apparently due to the fact that they were found in the same tombs and caves. With that said, however, we may also note that the young god, the male child of the goddess, never reaches adulthood, for there is no evidence of the existence of an adult male deity in Minoan religion. We can conclude that the relationship between the young god and the Goddess is not an expression of equality but rather one of service, with the young god paying homage to a greater power. It appears that this young god and his numerous manifestations as bull, goat, or ram still remained the "son" of the Goddess while personifying the dynamic vegetative life force that was also subject to annual death. In *Cretan Cults and Festivals*, Willetts says that, "the god represents the element of discontinuity, of growth, decay, and renewal in the vegetation cycle, as the goddess represents continuity. Because he shares in the mortality of the seed, he is an annually dying god."[9] The young Minoan god thus may well represent the so—called Year God whose annual rebirth was celebrated across the premodern world of the Near East, most notably in Mesopotamia.

Bulls and bullhorns had rich symbolic connotations and fulfilled many additional functions in Minoan religion. The crescent shaped bullhorn – one of the most prominent symbols of Minoan civilization – likely formed a frieze around the entire courtyard and along the walls of the palace of Knossos. The horns were placed on household shrines and on altars. Elaborate rhytons, or vessels, in the shape of a bull's head were used for pouring libations during sacred rituals. Schematized bullhorns served as altars consecrated to the Goddess. The horns of consecration marked the sanctity of an enclosure or the vicinity of a shrine or any other ritualistic object. Anointed with the blood of the bull, the horned altar also served as a foundation for the shaft of the double ax.

---

[9] Willetts, *Cretan Cults and Festivals*, p. 81.

Symbolic Connotations of the Minoan Bull Dance Ceremony

The most singular aspect of Minoan religion, however, was the ritualistic bull dance that was eventually performed in the central courts of the great temple complexes. The objective of the young dancers was *not* to conquer the bull but rather to adjust their own skills, senses, and movements to those of the animal, and, in the broadest sense, to tune into the rhythm of nature. The young men and women chosen for this ritual possessed well—built, athletic bodies, and they worked as a team. The famous bull dance fresco from the palace of Knossos provides a detailed visual of three performing acrobats: a young male and two young females. In the palace fresco, the young man grasps the horns of the charging animal, performing a somersault. While leaping over the animal's back, his hands pressed on the bull's spine. If everything went well, which was usually the case, the young athlete would land in the outstretched arms of his waiting companion. Another exquisite representation shows a bull with its forelegs resting on a large rectangular block with a young athlete vaulting through its horns. The young men are depicted with red—brownish complexion while the young women are light—skinned, allowing the observer to easily identify them. Very different from the well—known Spanish bullfight – in which the animal is seduced and infuriated by the red cape, eventually leading up to its cruel death celebrated as a victory *over* the bull – the Cretan bull leaping ceremony rather emphasized the supreme skills and graceful movements of the performing acrobats who entrusted their lives to one another. The frescoes at Knossos suggest that the young men and women may also have invoked the bull's magical power by vaulting over its back before the ceremonial slaying of the animal. Yet the final sacrifice of the bull to the

Minoan Goddess has to be interpreted rather as an act of reverence to the animal and the raw powers of nature that it embodied. As symbols of her regenerative powers, bulls and bullhorns were sacred to the Goddess since Neolithic times. Finally, the ritualistic bull dance may have served as a means of placating the earth, since it was understood that the Goddess could express her displeasure with devastating earthquakes.

The celebration of the Goddess reached its epiphany in Minoan culture. Her significance gradually declined during the later part of the second millennium BCE, reaching near—total extinction during the Iron Age in the first millennium BCE across the cultures.

The Role and Status of Women in Minoan Civilization

In a society in which the Goddess was highly revered, the question naturally arises: What was the role and status of women in ancient Crete? Minoan art and artifacts provide evidence of the prominent role that Cretan women played in this relatively free and prosperous society. Women played an active part in all aspects of life, were central to the culture, and had high status. Women were more commonly portrayed in Minoan arts and crafts than were their male counterparts. In the public sphere, females displayed an uninhibited, free—spirited, and lively attitude while mingling with males. A spirit of harmony and partnership between men and women, who were viewed as equal participants in life, appears to pervade the island culture. The partnership between the sexes characteristic of Minoan society is vividly illustrated in the aforementioned ritualistic bull dances performed by both males and females. Religion and entertainment were often interrelated, making Cretan leisure activities both meaningful and joyful. Music, singing, and dancing added to the pleasures of life, and numerous public ceremonies, processions, banquets, and acrobatic performances took place (bull leaping was the most prominent).

Minoan pottery shows that women had a passion for dancing in a ritualistic circle. In all premodern cultures, dance and its spiraling movements were a way of entering into communion with the Goddess. On the palace frescoes of Knossos, fashionable women with beautifully adorned hair arranged in long black ringlets display a great sense of elegance, refinement, and sophistication. Cretan clothing was typically designed for both aesthetic effect and practicality, allowing uninhibited freedom of movement. The ways in which men and women dressed and intermingled provides insight into the societal codes and norms of Minoan civilization. The frescoes express joyful and open—minded attitudes toward sexuality that, not surprisingly, correlate with the high status of women. The entire relationship between the sexes – both the definitions of gender roles and the fundamental attitude toward sexuality – was quite different from the values and paradigms of modern—day America in which, strangely enough, religious dogma tends to view sexuality, and even the mere display of naked female breasts, as more outrageous and "sinful" than violence. In contrast, the bare—breasted dress style of the women of Crete, and the skimpy clothes emphasizing the genitals of men in Minoan society, demonstrate a frank appreciation of sexual differences and of the pleasure that results from these differences.

Based on recent research conducted in the field of developmental psychology, we now know that this sort of lively and uninhibited interaction likely strengthened a sense of mutuality and partnership between men and women as individuals. Moreover, the free expression of sexuality likely led to a reduction of aggressive behavior patterns and may also have contributed to the generally peaceful and harmonious spirit that permeated Cretan life.

With that said, it is safe to conclude that women enjoyed high social, economic, political, and religious positions in Crete, and were active participants in every sphere of Minoan society. Women engaged in trade and also contributed to the rich variety of Minoan arts and crafts. In addition to the bull leaping, they were involved in all other forms of physical exercises and athletic performances. They likely served as priestesses, midwives, and healers. Evidence exists that the succession and inheritance passed through the female line, characteristic of any matrilineal society.

Was Minoan Civilization a Matriarchy Ruled by a Queen—Priestess?

With the role played by Minoan women so striking and diverse, the question arises: Was Minoan society a matriarchy ruled by a queen—priestess? While many feminist scholars view Minoan society (like Paleolithic and Neolithic cultures) to be prepatriarchal, matrifocal, and most likely matrilineal, the term "matriarchy" is in this context commonly rejected by scholars who are aware of its controversial history. The idea that matriarchy preceded patriarchy was originally proposed by historian J.J. Bachofen in his influential classic *Das Mutterrecht* (i.e.,The Mother Right), published in 1861. Bachofen uncovered important data, yet his theories are flawed by his conflation of matrilineal inheritance with the rule by women on the one hand, and by his assumption that patriarchy represents a higher stage of civilization on the other hand. Literally, matriarchy means rule of the mother or the mother principle. The term implies a society that is the opposite of patriarchy, namely, a society that is ruled by the fathers or the father principle. In *The Chalice and the Blade,* Riane Eisler points out that under the prevailing patriarchal paradigm, where ranking is the primary organizational principle, the notion of women enjoying a high status inevitably appears to suggest that men's status must be inferior and that ancient Crete was hence a matriarchal society. Yet the evidence of matrilineal descent and inheritance, as well as the existence of a predominant female deity, does *not* necessarily imply that Cretan society was matriarchal, nor "does it follow from the high status of Cretan women that the Cretan men had a status comparable to that of women in male—dominant social systems,"[10] as Eisler rightly observes. In *Rebirth of the Goddess*, Carol Christ seems to agree, stating that, "if matriarchy is the opposite of patriarchy then these societies (i.e., Minoan, Neolithic, and Paleolithic) should not be called matriarchies, since this would imply that they were large—scale class—and slave—based societies in which groups or classes of women ruled through control of the military."[11] Cretan women did not rule the island using armed force. We cannot be sure that a queen—priestess occupied the throne that was recovered at the palace of Knossos. Thus, we should probably refer to Minoan society as pre—patriarchal rather than as matriarchal.

Symbolic Connotations of the Labyrinth in Minoan and Classical Greek Mythology

One of the most popular mythic narratives passed down from classical Greece is the story of the labyrinth in Knossos built by the legendary architect Daedalus.

---

[10] Eisler, *The Chalice and the Blade*, p. 39.

[11] Christ, *Rebirth of the Goddess*, p. 59.

The labyrinth is one of the most ancient, contemplative, and transformational tools of humankind – it has been used for prayer, initiation, and psycho—spiritual growth for centuries. In the *The Mystic Spiral*, Jill Purce points out that the labyrinth is a representation of the cosmos, and, in the descending scale of analogy, "the world, the individual life, the temple, the womb...of the Mother (earth), the convolutions of the brain, the consciousness, the heart, the pilgrimage, the journey, and the Way."[12] In walking this archetypal map, we start at the perimeter. Walking the path of the labyrinth, like taking any journey, involves taking twists and turns, sometimes drawing near to and then away from the center – though the labyrinth's center signifies the core of our innermost being. The classical labyrinth differs considerably from the maze, which is a structure in which we can get lost, and which contains blind alleys and dead ends. In contrast, the path of a labyrinth always leads to its center.

A labyrinth was drawn on the ground floor corridor of the palace of Knossos. Similar labyrinths were found on Cretan coins and on seals from the palace of Hagia Triada. The Cretan labyrinth takes the walker through seven circuits before reaching its center. The term labyrinth is not Greek in origin, though we know that the affiliated word *labrys* refers to the double—headed ax. Therefore, the labyrinth is both the "House of the Double Ax" – that is, the temple of the Goddess where her mysteries were celebrated – and the place of spiritual rebirth. So how did the labyrinth in Knossos, the sanctuary of the Goddess, evolve into the place where the classical Greek hero Theseus killed the Minotaur, a creature with the head of a bull and a human body?

---

[12] Purce, *The Mystic Spiral*, p. 29.

The Slaying of the Great Goddess in Classical Greek Mythology and Beyond

According to the classical Greek narrative, Athens, a tributary of Crete, was forced to send seven young men and seven maidens every year to Knossos, in order to satisfy the rapacious appetite of a Minotaur who was kept hidden in the heart of the labyrinth. One year, Theseus, the son of the king of Athens, volunteered to go to Crete to kill the Minotaur that had been born of a union between King Minos' wife, queen Pasiphae, and a magnificent white bull that had emerged from the sea. With the aid of a ball of string given to Theseus by Ariadne, the daughter of King Minos (who had fallen in love with Theseus), Theseus found his way out of the labyrinth after slaying the bull—man. Of course, the ruling story exemplifies the Greek hero myth, in which Theseus slays the Minotaur in the dark underground labyrinth and liberates his country from a horrible annual tribute. But from a symbolic—metaphorical perspective, this narrative can be read as the archetypal drama that takes place in every human. Viewed from this perspective, Theseus is an embodiment of the archetypal masculine journey into the depths of the unknown and often terrifying dimensions of the psyche, eventually allowing the hero to find the treasure that lies at its core. Correspondingly, Ariadne's thread symbolizes the intuition of the archetypal feminine within each human, that guides the conscious mind through labyrinthine turnings and windings until it reaches the source of its being, after which this intuition can be trusted to lead us safely back.

Yet another interpretation of the same mythic narrative, suggested by some feminist scholars, is that the victory

of Theseus over the Minotaur signifies the metaphoric
deathblow to the ways of the Goddess. Theseus' story
is the myth of the patriarchal hero of classical Greece
who defies death by slaying the bull—man, ruler of the
underworld. The Athenian hero kills the Minotaur with
the double ax, emblem of the Goddess' womb, at the
center of the labyrinth. The sacred space deep within,
the "Holy of Holies" of the Goddess, was transformed
into the dreaded kingdom of the dead. Viewed from this
perspective, the violent act of Theseus is a complete
reversal of the paradigms of Minoan goddess culture
in which life and death are experienced as a sacred
interrelated whole and death is accepted as part of the life
cycle. Theseus usurped the powers of the Goddess, the
"Lady of the Labyrinth," and death was now no longer
viewed as integral part of the rebirth process in the body
of Gaia.

A similar narrative, which shows how the original
goddess—oriented values were modified during classical
Greek times to adopt new meanings more in accord with
patriarchal paradigms, is the story of the Delphic Oracle
ruled by the god Apollo. Archaeological evidence exists
that Apollo's shrine replaced an earlier sanctuary that
was previously dedicated to Gaia, the Earth. Delphi, which
is etymologically related to the word for womb, was
understood to be the "navel of the earth" in premodern
Greece. To justify Apollo's conquest of the site, the
Homeric hymn "To Pythian Apollo" (c.700—600 BCE)
states that Apollo, when he came to Delphi, slew a mighty
and savage female dragon that worked many evils on
people. This female dragon—serpent was sometimes also
referred to as guardian of the shrine of Mother Earth. The
description of Apollo's conquest of the Delphic dragon
evokes the *Enuma Elish*, the Babylonian creation myth
dating from the seventh century BCE. In this narrative,

Tiamat, the goddess of primordial chaos and the watery abyss, is portrayed as the source of evil and, perhaps not surprisingly, as a dragon—serpent. Similar to the bloody slaying of the Delphic dragon—serpent at the hands of Apollo, Tiamat is brutally slaughtered by the solar hero—god Marduk. The myth of Adam, Eve, and the serpent in Genesis can also be read as a narrative designed to denigrate the ancient goddesses. The same pattern of interpretation may be applied to those mythic narratives that report the slaying of dragons by Christian saints, as exemplified in the story of Saint George.

In yet another version of the patriarchal takeover myth, Zeus, the great "father god" of the Olympian family of Greek deities, kills the goddess Metis (whose name means, coincidentally, wisdom) by swallowing her. From this unusual union, the goddess Athena, fully armed and prepared for battle, is born from Zeus' head. In Aeschylus' play the *Oresteia*, Athena later proudly proclaims that no mother ever gave birth to her, thereby emphasizing the pseudo—biology proposed by this classical Greek narrative. And yet, even though Athena was eventually co—opted as a "warrior—goddess" in patriarchal classical Greek literature, she still retained some of the ancient symbols and qualities attributed to the great Goddess of Minoan and Neolithic cultures.

For example, one of her companion animals was the owl, and snakes protected her shield. The owl, the night bird and "Taker of Life" during the Neolithic period, eventually came to signify wisdom, which was another prominent feature of Athena.

Equally revealing are the mythic narratives reporting the numerous amorous escapades of the "sky—god" Zeus with countless goddesses, nymphs, and mortal women. In fact, Zeus' affairs regularly contributed to outbursts of rage and jealousy on the part of his "domesticated" wife, the "cow—eyed" goddess Hera, who may have been a faint and somewhat disempowered version of the great "Sky Cow" of ancient Egypt. Moreover, the historical timeline as well as the life—enhancing powers of the Minoan bull were perverted in those later narratives reporting how Zeus, disguised as a bull, raped the Phoenician princess Europa after carrying her across the Mediterranean all the way to the famous Cretan cave where the legendary king Minos was said to have been born from their union. We can easily see how in classical Greek mythology each of the goddesses is deprived of the powers she once possessed.

The same pattern is apparent in the mythic narrative of the Greek goddess Pandora, whose name means "Giver of All." This name may have reflected a faint memory of the life—sustaining gifts attributed to the Great Mother of the prehistoric period. Pandora is portrayed as a woman who opens a jar (often incorrectly translated as a box) and releases evil into the world rather than abundance and blessings.

The powers of the Goddess of pre—patriarchal cultures survived most prominently in the figure of Demeter, the great goddess of the harvest, whose story was celebrated for many centuries in the Eleusinian Mysteries. The classical Greek narrative has been passed down as the tale of Demeter and Persephone, her daughter, who dwelled in the realm of the dead during the winter months and returned to the earth to be united with her mother during the spring and summer seasons. It appears likely that the mythic narrative of Demeter and Persephone originated in ancient Crete. Similar to the ritualistic sacred marriage of the Near East, the celebration of Demeter's mysteries kept the spirit of the Great Goddess alive, yet her former powers were ultimately co—opted in the service of a new values system that reflected a radically different consciousness.

THE AFRICAN GODDESS OSHUN
– DANCING RIVER OF LIFE

"Brass and parrot feathers on a velvet skin.

White cowrie shells on black buttocks.

Oshun's eyes sparkle in the forest like the sun on the river.

She is the wisdom of the forest and of the river.

Where doctors fail, she cures with fresh water...

She feeds the barren woman with honey,

and her dry body swells up like a juicy coconut.

Oh, how sweet is the touch of a child's hand."[13]

The Yoruba goddess Oshun, whose name translates to "spring" or "source," has her origin in the cool springs at the source of the river in Oshogbo, Nigeria, that bears her name. Like all sweet river waters, Oshun brings life, abundance, and refreshment from the tropical sun to her people. She enchants those who approach her with her multi—faceted moods, functions, and personas. But, how does Oshun fit into the pantheon of African deities?

---

[13] Quoted from Monaghan, *The Goddess Companion*.

And what is her role within the broader context of African religion and the rich diversity of African culture?

Yoruba Civilization and the Ways of Spirit

Oshun's first worshipers were the ancestors of the Yoruba people of present—day Nigeria. Yoruba are brass and iron experts, weavers and dyers, and carvers of some of the finest sculpture arts in the world. They gained political importance in the seventeenth and eighteenth centuries as Yoruba trade routes spread over Western Africa. Recent archaeological research has shown that the Yoruba city of Ife dates back to the tenth century CE. The original Yoruba were farmers who cultivated large areas of their West African homeland – their abundant crops supported a complex urban civilization based on a system of city—states. But perhaps one of the greatest achievements of the Yoruba was the development of a subtle and complex religious way of life.

Prior to the white colonization of the continent, West Africans believed in an animated universe engaged in a process of continuous creation. Contrary to the still widespread misconceptions and stereotypical notions claiming that African religion is exclusively "polytheistic" and thus somewhat inferior or less evolved than the monotheistic traditions, the Yoruba basically acknowledge the existence of one supreme Ultimate Reality commonly referred to as Olodumare. Also called the "owner of all destinies," Olodumare is perceived as the ground of all being. From this Most High God all manifest forms come forth and ultimately return. The breath of this Supreme Reality is the source of all life in a universe that is conceived of as vibrant and engaged in an ongoing creative process. Olodumare is believed to be present in the world as a vital force called *ashe* by the Yoruba. This ever—unfolding life force, which is cyclical in nature and infuses all phenomena, is considered the driving principle of the evolutionary process. *Ashe* may also be compared to a divine energetic current that flows through many conductors – such as, for example, "human vessels" – of greater or lesser receptivity. Moreover, *ashe* finds its expression in the pantheon of deities or spirit beings that are referred to as *orisha*. These spirit beings are commonly perceived as different aspects of a singular concept of divinity.

Oshun Priestess Luisah Teish emphasizes in her book *Jambalaya*, that no image or gender for God exists in African religious thought. In fact, according to Teish, it is absurd to engage in discussions on gender as related to the divine. The Yoruba believe that having a particular image of God imposes an unduly human projection and limitation on the divine. God cannot be touched and God is certainly "no thing." The Yoruba realized that the things we say about God are limited by our individual perceptions of God, that is, our stage and structure of consciousness. Yet the divine is infinite. Everything we know is God, and that which we do not know is also God. In African belief, the divine makes itself known primarily through natural phenomena. As Teish puts it: "Knowable God is the sum total of all the forces of nature in dynamic interaction."[14] The Yoruba talk about the Supreme Being as the "Author of Day and Night" and the "Discerner of Hearts." The Yoruba believe that every human chooses his or her destiny and mental disposition with Olodumare as a witness prior to the individual's birth. This belief eventually explains why the Supreme Being is also referred to as the "owner of all destinies."

---

[14] Teish, *Jambalaya*, p. 54.

In times of difficulty and challenge, the Yoruba consult the priests or priestesses of a particular *orisha* and ask for assistance and guidance. According to the Yoruba religion, the world of spirit can be discerned in three ways or approaches. The first approach is via value systems that are based on honoring the ancestors. The second approach involves divination encoded within the larger cosmological framework. The third approach is the way of power commonly derived from the individual's relationship to the *orisha*. These three paths are in harmony with *ashe*, the divine life force. In our focus we will particularly emphasize the third approach, namely, the path to power through relationships with the *orisha*.

The Yoruba's first approach is based on the belief that *ashe* helps connect the past and present. Every generation owes its existence to the generations that precede it. The Yoruba venerate their ancestors because they acknowledge that the present community must look to the past for guidance on values and moral conduct. The experiences of the elders; and fundamental ethical precepts such as compassion, gentleness, and religious devotion; provide guidelines for the younger generations to grow in *ashe*. The Yoruba call their ancestors "People of Heaven." The reverence granted to their ancestors is expressed in invocations at family gatherings and religious ceremonies. Further, the Yoruba believe in reincarnation and the transmigration of souls. These beliefs are apparent in the names given to the living: The name Babatunde means "Father—returns," and Yetunde means "Mother—returns." The ancestors offer inspiration to their descendants, and they are viewed as a form of conscience. In revering their ancestors, the Yoruba appreciate their origins and ensure the continuity of their communities.

The Yoruba's second approach to the world of spirit is via divination. Ifa is the name of a technique of divination held in great esteem. Mastery of the technique requires ten to fifteen years of arduous training. The most respected Yoruba priests and priestesses are those who possess this knowledge. Through Ifa, the path of divination, the Yoruba can discern the will of Olodumare in all events and in the destiny affecting each human being. Ifa is a reflection of the divine order underlying the apparent chaos of the world in Yoruba belief. Sixteen, the number of cowrie shells or coconuts used for divination purposes, is the symbolic number of the cosmos representing the primeval order. The Yoruba believe that the world was created from an original palm tree that stood at the center of the world at Ile—Ife, their sacred city. The tree had sixteen branches forming the four cardinal points and the sixteen original quarters of Ile—Ife. The Yoruba palm tree is yet another version of the universal Word Tree, the *axis mundi*. The Ifa divination system is also closely affiliated with Yoruba history, religion, mythology, and folk medicine. The Yoruba regard Ifa as the repository of their beliefs and moral—ethical values. They use their divination system and the extensive poetic chants associated with it to validate important aspects of their culture. In Yoruba society, the authority of this system permeates every dimension of life because the Yoruba perceive Ifa as the voice of their deities and as an expression of the wisdom of their ancestors. This divination system also structures the worship of the *orisha*. In fact, we can say that the ceremonial life generated by Ifa constitutes the organizing principle of the religious vision of the Yoruba. Nearly all the offerings to the *orisha* are a result of divination. Ifa provides humans with information about their place in the world, their destiny, and what the deities require of them.

In Yoruba religion, nothing happens by chance, and it is the duty of humans to recognize this deeper truth and to align themselves with the great mystery. To grow in *ashe* means to respect the elders, to seek oracular guidance, and to properly honor the *orisha*, who are considered to be personifications of *ashe* as expressed through the forces of nature. The Ifa priesthood is responsible for directing supplicants to the proper *orisha*. This brings us to the third approach.

This approach to power is through a relationship with an *orisha*. The nature of the relationship between the *orisha* and humans is both intimate and reciprocal. Humans offer sacrifices such as animals and plants to the *orisha* at shrines erected to honor them – the Yoruba believe that the *orisha* would wither and die without the *ashe* of sacrifices, for the *orisha* are not immortal. This fact clearly reveals that both humans and *orisha* experience limitations and boundaries. In order to be effective, the *orisha* have to be nourished.

Each *orisha* has his or her favorite sacrificial food, which is consecrated to the *orisha* and consumed by the devotees at ceremonies. The *orisha*, invigorated by the blood of sacrifices, are in turn expected to provide assistance to their followers who are experiencing challenging life circumstances. For every important activity or aspect of life, a particular *orisha*, whose power is believed to underlie it, is implored. The *orisha* Ogun, for example, is the patron of smiths, helping them to unlock the secrets of the earth and forge metals into tools that can be used for both warfare and agricultural purposes. Ogun can also be viewed as the vital force or *ashe* of iron itself. Another example is Shango, who is affiliated with the power of lightning, thunder, and kingship. Each *orisha* possesses specific character traits and is identified with particular natural phenomena. Orisha are manifestations of the whole of creation. They each offer a different path to wisdom, health, and success. Yet from a mystical— esoteric perspective, each *orisha* also has an archetypal dimension and represents an internal quality. This quality is identified with a specific energetic pattern that is reflected in natural phenomena and in human consciousness.

These patterns are an expression of *ashe*, the divine life force. Adepts are able to recognize these energetic currents that infuse all of creation and can be channeled in sacred ceremony.

Traditionally, the Yoruba recognize as many as 1,700 *orisha*, though only a few have achieved prominence. The great *orisha* are attended to by dedicated priests and priestesses, who act as keepers of Yoruba religion. This priesthood has to undergo an extensive and thorough training in dance styles, songs of prayer, and herbal healings. Each of the *orisha* has his or her favorite song, dance, rhythm, musical instrument, herbs and sacrificial food. By knowing how to make the *orisha's ashe* present in those who consult them, priests and priestesses contribute to the growth and health of their community. The Yoruba believe that the *orisha* originally came into this world in the holy city of Ile Ife, and that this was also the place where they introduced crafts such as metallurgy and farming, and spiritual practices such as divination. We will now turn our attention more extensively to the goddess Oshun, one of the most popular *orisha* of the Yoruba.

Oshun – Goddess of Many Titles, Moods, and Functions

Oshun the "source" is the nurturing mother, feminine seductress, beautiful enchantress, fierce protectress,

powerful leader, wise counselor and diviner, giver of
life and fertility, healer, and, finally, the mother of the
African fresh waters – to name just the most important of
her numerous features and manifestations.

Oshun's Role in the Cosmological Vision of the Yoruba

Oshun's importance within Yoruba cosmology is
emphasized in their creation narrative. She is believed
to have been the only female among the first seventeen
orishas to descend from the spirit realms to assist in the
process of creating a habitable world. At first the sixteen
male *orisha* ignored Oshun because of her gender. Then
they were advised by Olodumare to consult with her.
They ended up apologizing for their offensive actions
and offering a sacrifice to Oshun. As compensation, the
goddess demanded that all the women who, like herself,
possessed great internal strength and extraordinary
courage, would receive permission to be initiated into
the ways of male power. Not surprisingly, Oshun came
to be regarded as the ancestor and leader of Yoruba
women, and she continues to serve as a source of female
empowerment and authority.

Oshun's participation in the task of organizing and
maintaining a habitable world for humans is related to
her function as a diviner. Ifa is one of the three primary
pathways of being in perfect alignment with *ashe*; and
Oshun's first husband, the powerful Orunmila, is the
wise guardian of the Ifa oracle who possesses the full
knowledge of the art of divination. The Yoruba believe
that the art of mastering the sixteen cowries divination
system was transmitted to Oshun by Orunmila, the carrier
of both the wisdom to unveil the forces at work against an
individual and of the knowledge required to placate those
powers. In Yoruba cosmology, these forces are represented

by the *aje*, powerful beings that are an expression of the spectrum of life's potentialities. This knowledge allows the *aje* to influence natural events and affect human lives.

Oshun is the leader of the *aje*, and in this particular role she has to protect the covenants that seal the benevolent and/or malevolent actions of the *aje*. As the keeper of these secret covenants, Oshun possesses the power to bind or loosen these covenants. But as an *orisha*, Oshun remains a benefactor to humanity – for her to initiate destructive action would be tantamount to her own annihilation. In this context, we may also note that in Yoruba metaphysics seemingly opposite forces are viewed as complementary, rather than as dualistic (as in the "dualistic" concept of "good" versus "evil.") Every individual has his or her own power that can be used for beneficial or malevolent actions.

As the leader of the powerful *aje* and keeper of these secret covenants, Oshun contains enormous intrinsic power. In *Oshun Seegesi*, African American scholar Diedre Badejo emphasizes that Oshuns' knowledge of divination is both acquired and inherent. One of Oshun's symbols, the beaded comb, may be understood in this context. The Yoruba believe that the goddess uses this comb to part the pathways that lead to either a human or divine existence. One of her multiple appellations, *Oshun Seegesi Olooya— iyun*, refers to this particular role and is best translated as "owner of the flawless and perfectly carved beaded comb."

To conclude, Oshun's marriage to Orunmila reflects balance and reciprocity, suggesting that intrinsic wisdom and knowledge of the powerful forces shaping human lives are qualities shared by both male *and* female.

Oshun – River Mother and Fertility Icon

Yoruba mythology tells us that Oshun has her origins
in the sparkling headwaters of the river that bears her
name in Nigeria. As Luisah Teish points out, the Yoruba
observed the voluptuous river with its sweet water and
beautiful stones and surmised intuitively that it was
female. As the patroness of the fresh river waters from
which she was born, Oshun embodies the cooling *ashe* of
the water itself, providing her people with good health
and vitality. In her form as the mother of the salt waters,
she is known as Yemaya. As the source of all the waters,
she is the yielding force that is akin to the yin principle
in Chinese Daoism. In fact, in Yoruba understanding,
Oshun is the invisible mother present at every gathering
because she represents the cosmological forces of water
and moisture. Viewed as omnipresent and omnipotent,
her power finds its expression in a Yoruba proverb,
reminding us that everyone has a vital need of fresh
water and hence should revere her. At the annual Oshun
festival still celebrated in modern—day Nigeria, sacrificial
offerings are carried to a specific location on the banks of
her river. These offerings commonly include honey, mead,
oranges, pumpkins, sweets, incense, and essential oils.
Sacrificial offerings serve the broader purpose of placating
malevolent forces that threaten the survival of humankind
and the emergence of a new life cycle. The offerings are
viewed as indispensable to the proper maintenance of
cosmic harmony, balance, and ritual efficacy. Once the
festival procession reaches the banks of the river, Oshun's
spirit is invoked. Her acceptance of these offerings is
considered a good portent. Some people bathe their
faces in the river or taste its cool sweetness. Others fill
assorted containers with the sacred water, which they use
throughout the year for ritual and medicinal purposes.
One of Oshun's emblems is a pottery dish filled with

white stones from a river's bed. Moreover, as the source of all the fresh waters, the goddess is affiliated with the principle of universal order and harmony.

According to the Yoruba creation narrative, when the male *orisha* first attempted to subjugate Oshun because of her gender, she withdrew her divine participation in the process of creation and this led to a fundamental imbalance. The evolutionary process was only allowed to resume after the necessary amends had been made for this omission. This mythic narrative clearly implies that any attempt to organize the world without female participation leads to inertia and violates the laws of the universe as envisioned by the Supreme Being. The narrative further suggests that activating powers reside in the female principle because it ushers in new life.

Oshun is also revered as *Yeye*, referring to her role as the nurturing cosmic mother who protects her people. In fact, the cosmological vision of the Yoruba asserts Oshun's powerful role as the one who "expels the breathing human form through her womb thus forcing it to live... and to experience the trauma and joy of birth."[15] As a woman who knows the agony of giving birth to humanity, Oshun naturally bonds with all women who experience the joy and pain in childbirth. In the context of her maternal function, she is also the giver of fertility who possesses the power to bless her devotees with children. In addition to helping barren women to conceive, Oshun is a healer of the female reproductive organs, and assists with ovarian and uterine problems. Herbal infusions sacred to the *orisha* are commonly used for such healing purposes. The properties of certain herbs viewed as being infused with the divine life force are among the most

---

[15] Badejo, *Oshun Seegesi*, p. 74.

closely guarded secrets of Yoruba priests and priestesses. Oshun herself is praised as a supreme herbalist, who possesses the knowledge of medicines that are particularly beneficial for childbearing women. Female devotees call on her to help with complications during pregnancy and delivery, and the symbolic references between the sweet waters and the amniotic fluid are evident. The image of a human embryo floating in the watery womb is found in bold relief on the walls of the Oshun grove in Oshogbo. Many mythic narratives liken the river waters to Oshun's generative womb and recognize the goddess as the mother of all the creatures drawing their life from fresh waters.

Oshun is also related to the fish, a fertility symbol dating from the Neolithic that appears across many cultures. As the goddess of fertility, Oshun herself is said to have given birth to numerous children from her love affairs with a series of male deities. Yet as a female *orisha*, she maintains her intrinsic powers. Considered to be the mother of the first legendary kings, she is also believed to have given birth to the divine twins of the Yoruba pantheon, the Ibeji. Twins are generally considered to be a living expression of divine favor and special powers. They are celebrated every year, and many twins and their mothers are ardent devotees of Oshun. With a history of high infant mortality rates and frequent miscarriages due partly to infectious diseases, fertility and reproduction play an extremely critical role in the lives of the Yoruba. Childlessness and infertility are regarded as major tragedies. The desire for increased fertility may also have historical roots in the brutal slave—raids launched by Europeans in the early nineteenth century, and in the disastrous internecine wars partly fueled by the raids and kidnapping campaigns.

Oshun's power is based on her being the goddess of fertility. Yet the Yoruba pay homage to Oshun as both the provider of children and the warrior—goddess who fiercely protects her children from the devastations of drought, warfare, and social injustice. In this context, it is important to remember Oshun's broader role within the cosmological vision of the Yoruba. As the goddess of fertility, Oshun plays a crucial role in the perpetuation of the ever—unfolding cycle of life and death that connects the ancestors, those who are currently living, and generations yet to be born. Oshun's womb is the quintessential matrix that nurtures myriad potentialities and holds the key to the miracle of life. Yoruba women mirror Oshun's vital contribution within the broader universal framework, for without their participation the continuity of human life and progress would cease.

Oshun Iyalode

In addition to her participation in the creation of the world and her role as the provider of fertility and children, Oshun is also known as *Yalode*, the mother of prosperity and abundance. Marriage, childbirth, naming ceremonies, and childrearing require a steady source of monetary income, so when the Yoruba pray for children, they also pray for the prosperity to fulfill their social obligations. Conversely, later on, children are expected to provide for the needs of their elderly parents, especially for those of their mother. Women with superb business skills are viewed as exceedingly good mothers because they can benefit their children and extended families. Consequently, Oshun also acts as the patroness of craftswomen, female traders, and entrepreneurs. She bestows economic success on her female devotees. Historically, this particular function of Oshun may have originated during a period in which the town Oshogbo, home of her sanctuary, experienced rapid commercial growth and prosperity due to its strategic location at the intersection of important West African trade routes. Given its rich natural resources, Oshogbo town was an ideal setting for the development of arts, crafts, and local trade since the fifteenth century CE. Most of Oshun's devotees are organized in guilds of craftswomen, a factor that greatly enhances female group solidarity and fosters the economic independence of Yoruba women. As the progenitor ruler of the Yoruba and the leader of the powerful beings known as *aje*, Oshun's function as an embodiment of female power and leadership is repeatedly affirmed. The profuse oral literary references to Oshun as an *oba*, a ruler and warrior, certainly confirm her leadership function. In *Oshun Seegesi,* scholar Diedre Badejo opines that the name Oshun served as a title for the ruler of women, which may have preceded male leadership. Badejo also suggests that female rule may have been prevalent in Oshogbo during the period from the early 1600s to the late 1800s.

Oshun's role as the patroness of craftswomen and the protectress of the interests of market women, as well as her function as a model of female leadership, are an expression of the interrelatedness between local market economies, political leadership, and religious practices in Yoruba society.

Oshun – The Supreme Enchantress

Oshun is also the goddess of love and beauty. In this function, she embodies the archetype of the seductive enchantress and is similar to the nymphs and sirens of Western folktale traditions. Oshun is viewed as the consort of various male deities of the Yoruba pantheon – but none are able to hold her for any length of time. Her desires are too refined and her love too overflowing to be confined by the conventions of marriage. Oshun's extraordinary powers of attraction, together with her love of sensual pleasures, establish her as a great coquette. She brazenly flirts with men and delights in their seduction. Oshun embodies the vital spark of erotic attraction between humans that is an underlying and ever—present aspect of the mystery of life. In the African diaspora in Cuba, Oshun's promiscuity and her sophistication in the arts of love earned her the somewhat ambiguous and problematic epithet of *puta santa*, that is, the "whore—saint." Interestingly, this characterization juxtaposes two of the most powerful and paradoxical aspects of femininity.

Correspondences between Oshun and the Roman Catholic Virgin Mary

Evidence exists that the Cuban perception of Oshun as a saint – in addition to her sensual and flirtatious ways – was likely influenced by the concept of the Virgin Mary in Roman Catholicism, which was introduced to the New World with the arrival of Spanish missionaries in the sixteenth century CE. Like the Virgin Mary, Oshun is a carrier of primordial wisdom and a saintly healer who prescribes remedies for the sick. The "saint" and the "whore" are thus not necessarily perceived as incompatible polar opposites in the African diaspora in Cuba. Yet when examining the Christian tradition, it is apparent that the exclusivist perception of the female through the dualistic lens of either saint or whore is much more pronounced.

The Book of Thunder, which is part of the noncanonical scriptures dating from the period of early Christianity, may serve as an example. In Thunder, a female voice

representing Wisdom engages in lamentations in which
she points to the dualistic stereotypical notions of
"saint" and "whore" through which she is commonly
perceived. Another example of this perception is the
sharp juxtaposition of the Virgin Mary with the notion of
the "witch" in the Roman Catholic tradition. During the
Christian Inquisition in Europe, hundred thousands of
women (estimates vary) were accused of worshiping the
devil and engaging in sexual intercourse with him. Most
of these women were persecuted, tortured, and burned at
the stake, especially at the height of the witchhunts from
the early sixteenth to the late seventeenth centuries CE.
The image of the witch appears also in Yoruba esoteric
teachings, where Oshun *Ibu Ikole* – which means Oshun
"the vulture," and is another image evocative of Neolithic
bird goddesses – is affiliated with witchcraft. This idea
derives from Oshun's role as the leader of the powerful
beings called aje in Yoruba metaphysics, and may also
be related to her supreme skills as an herbalist. With
that said, however, it needs to be emphasized that the
term "witch" carries much more positive connotations
in the African traditions than it does in mainstream
Western culture.

Witchcraft in Africa is a sophisticated science practiced
by those with the necessary skills. This science is said to
be so powerful that the adepts are reputed to have power
over life and death. Oshun assumes the role of the "queen
of witches" in the later Lukumi tradition in Cuba, where
witchcraft is viewed in a positive light as well.

Yoruba Religious Beliefs and the Development of Santeria

When the Yoruba were enslaved in great numbers and
shipped to the plantations of Cuba and Brazil in the

early nineteenth century, they brought their African religion with them. This gave them the necessary comfort and strength to endure the unimaginable hardship of slavery. The Yoruba slaves called their African deities *santos*, saints, and they found ways of venerating them in Christian churches. Yet at the same time, they were forced to disguise their ancestral rituals and to embrace the religion of their oppressors. Ultimately, descendents of the Yoruba never ceased to worship their deities with the songs and dances from the African motherland. The new syncretistic tradition that emerged in the Americas is referred to as Santeria, namely, the "way of the saints." The necessity to disguise their rituals and practices in order to protect their African religion from Christian persecution has, not surprisingly, created numerous distortions and misconceptions. Even today, Santeria is sometimes confused with sensationalist images of sorcery fueled by headlines such as "Blood Cults spread through U.S." The juxtaposition of the Virgin Mary with the image of the witch in the history of Western Christianity may also have helped to shape the notion of Oshun as the "whore—saint" in the New World. In Santeria, however, this allegedly incompatible polarity gets resolved in the realization that both aspects are ultimately two sides of one and the same coin. Each "opposite" contains the essence of the other within its nature. Finally, it is important to note that Oshun's devotees are wary of the problematic perception of the goddess as a "whore—saint," for they argue that Oshun grants her favors only for love. This clearly excludes the connotations evoked by the common understanding of the term "prostitute" in our times.

In the Cuban Yoruba tradition, Oshun is celebrated particularly in her role as the supreme enchantress and irresistible seductress. She loves fancy gowns of

yellow silk and white—checked cotton, and often carries
a fan or a peacock feather. Oshun adorns herself with
jewelry of corals, amber, and all types of red metals such
as copper, brass, and gold. She loves to receive gifts such
as silk textiles, perfume, honey, and sweet foods. Mythic
narratives portray her winning the hearts of men by her
songs that evoke the murmur of watery currents. Oshun
also captivates her devotees by swaying her arms in
slow rhythms and by jangling her gold bracelets, thereby
emulating the river. Her most seductive expression is
in her dance, which is accompanied by ritual drumming
and chanting. The movements of the dancers within the
complex and nuanced rhythms reveal the *orisha's* vital
force, his or her *ashe*. The devotee experiences the *orisha*
less as an external entity but rather as an intrinsic
divine quality.

For spiritual aspirants, personal growth is marked by
progressive stages of initiation culminating in that of
orisha priesthood, when the devotee becomes an *olorisha*,
that is, one who "owns" or "possesses" an *orisha*. The
orisha are believed to descend and seize the body of the
dancer, similar to a rider who takes command of a horse.
Yet Yoruba mysticism equally emphasizes that the *orisha*
is indwelling, allowing the dancer to enter an altered state
of consciousness. When the devotee becomes an *olorisha*,
the *orisha* that has been recognized and consecrated
within him or her is made responsive to certain songs and
drum rhythms. When the proper ceremonial setting is in
place, the *olorisha* goes into a profound trance. Eventually,
the *orisha* emerges through the human medium to both
dance and speak with the assembled devotees. The actions
performed by the medium – from simple gestures to
pantomimed dramas – are immediately recognizable to
the community as reenactments of mythological episodes

and ritual objects relating to the life of a particular *orisha*. Yoruba ceremony, in particular dance, makes the divinities present in the human world in dramatic ways.

The Sensual and Spiritual Power of Oshun's Dance

Roughly three principal stages of Oshun's dance can be discerned. In the first stage, Oshun dances the rhythms of the river of her birth by swaying from side to side in languid motions, sometimes spilling forward at rapids or spiraling gently in the backwaters. At times she raises her arms and shakes her bracelets like the bubbling of springs. At other times she allows her arms to cascade down along her body. She seems to undulate vertically and repeatedly from the pelvic area up through the chest, shoulders, neck, and head. The second stage recounts Oshun taking her bath, frolicking in the river waters and pampering herself with fragrant soaps and precious oils. She combs her hair and contemplates her reflection on the surface of the water. The third and final stage takes Oshun back into the community where she plays the coquette. Her body struts and sways, and she kisses and laughs provokingly into her audience.

In her rhythmic movements, Oshun emulates the sacred river that bears her name; but she also celebrates her physicality and its sensuous, beautiful, and alluring aspects – drawing community attention to the female body itself. Oshun's dance is first of all an invocation of all aspects of womanhood. And, as in all *orisha* dance performances, transformation takes place. Worshipers are transformed into the divinity through the recognition of complementary relationships that honor the interrelatedness of movement, instrumental sound, and spiritual energy. The heightened awareness of all the senses allows for new channels and dimensions to open as the performance unfolds. In *Dancing Wisdom*, Yvonne Daniel observes: "As worshipers imitate and perform Oshun's dance sequences repeatedly, they deepen into her spiritual essence with matching energy. Oshun's dance becomes not only an invocation for the essence of vibrant female energy but also a public display for the admiration and adoration of the female gender and female body form. Within the gestures of Oshun, the viewer sees the Yoruba concepts of beauty, grace, and femininity...Oshun's beauty is openness, independence, alertness, and an empowered sense of self."[16]

Gender and Power as Expressed in the Worship of Oshun

The role of Yoruba women as powerful icons central to communal harmony and wellbeing is as ancient as it is contemporary. In traditional African thought, female empowerment originates from the supreme source, just as male authority does. Like their male counterparts, Yoruba women are believed to be born with *ashe*, the divine vital force that permeates creation including what we may refer to as personal power. We may note that the manifestation of *ashe* as personal power is not viewed in terms of gender by the Yoruba; rather than through a gender—specific lens, it is perceived as *human* power. Ultimately, male and female are viewed as complementary principles of the cosmic and the social order. And female power is considered to be intrinsic, authentic, and autonomous in its essence. As custodians of the earth, the fire, the water, and the wood, women are, from a metaphysical perspective, agents of change gifted with the ability to transform natural elements into tools of sustenance. The narrative poems of the Ifa divination corpus demonstrate

---

[16] Daniel, *Dancing Wisdom*, p. 259.

the crucial role of women in planning, maintaining, and directing socio—political and religious interactions. The structures of Yoruba religion reflect and even partly institutionalize the political system. This interrelatedness between religious and political structures is dramatically illustrated in the role of Oshun's chief priestess, the *Iya Oshun Oshogbo*. This title refers to both religious and political positions of female leadership. For example, the chief priestess of Oshun officiates at the four—days weekly worship of the goddess and at Oshun's invocation to her annual festival. Yet at the same time, the Iya Oshun assumes a more political role as the "official mother" of the local political ruler of Oshogbo, the *Ataoja.* In other terms, Oshun – in the person of her chief priestess – co—rules Oshogbo with the local tutelary male ruler, who also performs sacred rituals. The dual political and religious responsibilities are on display during the annual Oshun festival, when the *Ataoja* and the Iya Oshun perform the sacred rites in each other's presence. Both officials are expected to minister to the political and spiritual needs of the Yoruba. The *Ataoja* and the Iya Oshun are considered to be the trustees of the people's intent to survive. They symbolize the religio—political order that serves the needs of the community. Hence, the positions of the Iya Oshun and the *Ataoja* represent the socio—cultural stability and political continuity that underlie communal wellbeing. In the context of the chief priestess' function as the "official mother" of the local political ruler, we may note that the Egyptian goddess Isis was also viewed as the mother, and source of power, of the ruler. In the case of Egypt this was the pharaoh, who was believed "to sit on her lap," that is, on her throne.

As the head of the religious hierarchy of Oshun functionaries, the chief priestess directs the senior priest, who is ranked second and assists her in carrying the sacrificial offerings to the river during the annual Oshun festival. Interestingly, this is the only title in the hierarchy of Oshun worship that is held by a man, although women *and* men alike are devotees of Oshun. Third in rank to the Iya Oshun is the female Balogun Oshun. *Balogun* means commander—in—chief and is another important political title, suggesting that the *balogun* has the ability to engage in physical confrontation if necessary. The function of the *balogun* is evocative of Oshun's role as a fierce warrioress who, like the Hindu goddesses Kali and Durga, protects her children from danger. The Balogun Oshun serves as the bodyguard who leads the procession of male devotees during the festival. She is in charge of the preparations for the festival and takes care of the Oshun shrine. Another example is the *Arugba*, the virgin sacrifice—carrier, who takes the offering to the river during the festival. The *Arugba* is chosen from the close relatives of the local ruler and formerly had to live with the Iya Oshun. Today, the *Arugba* attends school, but she must live in the Oshun shrine for one month every year. From the time she is chosen until her marriage, the *Arugba* must not carry anything on her head except the calabash containing the annual offering to Oshun. When she is married, the *Arugba* remains a devotee of the *orisha,* and her husband is bound to fulfill her ritualistic obligations when she is incapacitated. Similarly, for all the devotees and priestesses of Oshun, marriage enhances rather than limits their ritual duties and roles within the religious hierarchy, for they too will eventually become mothers.

Oshun's oracle, the sixteen—cowries divination, is used to select both the Iya Oshun and the *Arugba*. Both women are accorded special economic and social privileges such as first choice of the provisions from the market without compensation to the sellers. This privilege reaffirms the role of Oshun's chief priestess as the *Iyalode*, "mother of the outdoors," that is, the markets. In general, the same title is also conferred upon the female leaders of women's organizations.

In sum, the position of the Iya Oshun is an excellent example of Yoruba women's integral role in the vision and maintenance of their communities. It is just another expression of the interrelatedness of the political, religious, and economic structures in Yoruba society. While Yoruba society is clearly patriarchal with land and other forms of inheritance remaining with the paternal line, the oral literature and the mythology of Oshun demonstrate that the concept of organized sisterhood operates astonishingly well within the overall societal framework. This concept also defines the art of mothering in Yoruba culture in which co—wives are also co—mothers in polygynous households and extended families. The coordination of familial and communal activities at birth, naming ceremonies, marriages, festivals, and funerals embodies the principles of social cohesion and the primacy of female organizational expertise. Like Iyalode Oshun, women leaders organize large numbers of females around specific tasks and events.

Sisterhood and female solidarity are also displayed prominently at the annual festival dedicated to the worship of Oshun. This festival provides an ideal public forum to express all sorts of female concerns and grievances. During this occasion, women devotees and priestesses of Oshun raise their voices both in praise of the *orisha* and in social protest. The voices of the disenfranchised and disaffected are represented as well as those of childless women, refugees of war, drought, and disease, along with the food—sellers and the new mothers who are singing in a grand display of all the paradoxes within the human condition.

One of the prime grievances addressed by these women is sexism. While male sexism is clearly present in Yoruba society, it is both acknowledged and challenged. For example, a line from one of the festival songs clearly ridicules and dismisses male sexism with the following words: "We are members of the group. Boys who do not like us should sit (stay behind)."[17] Sexism needs to be addressed since it threatens the vibrancy of the human community to which Oshun and her sisters give birth. African women do have the power to challenge any threat to the social order. In light of the Yoruba creation narrative, which recounts how the male *orishas'* attempt to negate Oshun threatened to destroy humanity, it's been illustrated that male domination and sexism generate chaos and, ultimately, can cause an intolerable imbalance. This belief system encourages Yoruba men to come to terms with female empowerment within the overall patriarchal framework of Yoruba society.

With all that said, it appears that Yoruba gender roles are complementary rather than antagonistic. The mythology of Oshun and the oral literature focused on her worship provide evidence that reciprocity and a balance of the archetypal masculine and feminine are woven into the fabric of Yoruba culture. The orisha Oshun emanates her *ashe*, her life force, as a deity and as a human being. She is indeed the quintessential matrix and a source of female empowerment and leadership, as her numerous titles, attributes, and deeds indicate. Officials who carry Oshun's name in their titles are treated with reverence and respect. The titles that refer to her

---

[17] Quoted from Badejo, *Oshun Seegesi*, p.165.

numerous roles and functions express an ideal of parity between the sexes within the sociopolitical and religious structures of Yoruba culture.

THE VIRGIN MARY –
RETURN OF THE GODDESS?

Hail Mary, full of grace,

Our Lord is with you.

Blessed are you among women,

and blessed is the fruit of your womb.

Holy Mary, Mother of God,

pray for us sinners,

now and at the hour of our death.

(Luke 1:26–35, 42–48)

At the heart of the devotion to Mother Mary lies the Hail Mary, the most enduring prayer of the rosary dedicated to her. During the two thousand years of Christian history, the veneration of Mary has developed in different ways. High points of Marian piety can be found in the medieval and baroque periods, and in the Orthodox and Roman Catholic traditions, while modern Protestantism has tended to minimize her powers and her role in the divine realm. The Protestant churches have never accepted the doctrines of Assumption and Immaculate Conception considered the cornerstone of Marian theology in the Orthodox and Roman Catholic traditions. During the twelfth and thirteenth centuries, glorious cathedrals were built in honor of Our Lady along pilgrimage routes in France and Germany, in particular the Gothic cathedrals of Chartres and Notre Dame of Paris. Some of these cathedrals were built around relics such as bits of hair or pieces of clothing allegedly left behind at the Assumption.

Popular medieval tradition invested Mary with the power to work miracles. One motif that frequently appeared in her narrative is the power of her breast milk to cure blindness, cancer, and other illnesses. Contemplative men and women saw Mary in visions and dedicated their lives to her service. Hymns celebrated all aspects of her life, from her own conception, to the birth of Jesus, and, finally, her assumption and enthronement as the new "Queen of Heaven." Yet Marian shrines and pilgrimage sites are by no means limited to medieval Christianity. In fact, the three most prominent "apparitional" shrines dedicated to the cult of the Virgin – Guadalupe (Mexico), Lourdes (France), and Fatima (Portugal) – came into being in the sixteenth, nineteenth, and twentieth centuries. Indeed, in our modern and postmodern times, belief in the power of Mary has experienced a renaissance.

In *The Myth of the Goddess,* Anne Baring and Jules Cashford refer to Mary as the unrecognized Mother goddess of the Christian tradition. Andrew Harvey observes in the *Essential Mystics* that "one of the most significant results of the reemergence of the Sacred Feminine in our times is that Mary is being increasingly turned to not merely as the Mother of God but as the most poignant of all of humanity's images of the divine Mother."[18] But what do we really know about the mother of Jesus Christ, and what do the Gospels tell us about her? What is her position within the overall framework of Christian theology? What are her symbols and functions? Can Mary be considered an expression of the reemergence of the powerful pre—Christian goddesses?

---

[18] Harvey, *Essential Mystics*, p.169.

What Do We Know about the Mother of Jesus?

Little is known about the historical woman Mary of Nazareth. Biblical references to Mary were considered by early Christians to be an inadequate testimony to the life of the mother of Jesus. The New Testament does not provide any facts whatsoever about Mary's birth and the exact nature of her relationship with Joseph. In the first centuries CE, as devotion to Mary was finding a place in the body of Christian beliefs, speculation about Mary's life gave rise to a collection of popular stories that, in effect, fill in some of the blanks of the biblical accounts. These tales are an integral part of ancient texts known as pseudepigraphical scriptures, that is, writings that bear an obviously false claim of authorship.

Two of these traditions are especially important for the development of Marian devotion: the stories relating to Mary's birth, and those recalling her death. In a text known as the Proevangelium of James (c. 150 CE), a book that purports to have been written by Jesus' brother James, Mary's parents Joachim and Anna are introduced as a rich and pious yet childless couple. After prayers and supplications, both receive angelic revelations that they will have a child. They vow to commit the child to a life of temple service. The pseudepigraphical traditions stress Mary's own miraculous birth, which brought her life into congruence with that of her son. When Mary is finally born, she shows a precocious piety and is duly dedicated as a perpetual virgin. Mary's birth narrative clearly derives from the motivation to define the Virgin's nature as sanctified and to set her apart from other women. In theological terms, this meant that the body from which Christ was born also had to be brought into the world accompanied by special signs. Similarly, Mary's body could not have suffered common corruption after death.

The message of the Marian pseudepigrapha is basically that Mary neither was born nor died in the way of other human beings.

How do the canonical Gospels portray Mary? In the New Testament, Mary is only a human woman, who found favor with God. All stories about her agree that she is the mother of Jesus. But some of the few references to her in the Gospels of Mark, Luke, and Matthew – aside from the infancy narratives of Matthew and Luke – seem to reflect a tradition that positions Mary and Jesus' siblings as unbelievers who are affiliated with the reluctant hometown community of Nazareth. Mark even goes as far as to describe this local community as seeking to seize Jesus, believing him to be mad in one particular incident. Jesus' mother and brothers then come and, standing outside, ask to speak to him. Jesus repudiates them, identifying his followers – and not his biological family – as his "true mothers and brothers" (Mark 3:21, 31—35). Matthew and Luke repeat the same story with variations. In contrast to Mark, however, Mary appears to play a role that is more supportive of Jesus in the Gospel of John. She intervenes, for example, at the marriage feast at Cana (2:1—11) where she asks Jesus to do something about the dwindling supply of wine. At first, Jesus rejects her request, but later he orders the water jars used for Jewish rites of purification to be filled with water, which he eventually turns into wine. The implicit message of John is that Jesus is the "new wine" that will eventually supersede the old, inefficacious rites. This particular passage portrays Mary rather as a partner in the mysterious unfolding of the true nature of her son. Moreover, during Jesus' last hours, his mother reappears at the foot of the cross, along with several women disciples. Jesus entrusts her to the care of the "beloved disciple." It is interesting to note that Mary's appearance next to the cross is only reported in John (19:25 —27). Because Mary remains, generally speaking, a minor figure in the canonical Gospels, this chapter focuses primarily on the two core issues of Marian theology concerned with her official status within the church tradition: the Virgin Birth and the Assumption.

The Virgin Birth

Because the theme of the Virgin Birth stands at the beginning of Christian theology and became a doctrine in the mid—nineteenth century, it deserves a more detailed elaboration. The tradition of Mary's virginal conception appears in the infancy narratives added to the Gospels of Matthew and Luke. According to the Gospel of Luke (1:26—38), Mary was a virgin engaged to a man named Joseph when she received a visitation from the archangel Gabriel. The angel announces to her that she has been chosen by God to be the mother of a son conceived by the Holy Spirit: "The Holy Spirit will come upon you, and the power of the Most High will overshadow you; for that reason the holy child to be born will be called Son of God" (Luke 1:35). Interestingly, it is Mary who is an active agent in the miraculous conception in Luke's infancy narrative. In contrast to the Gospel of Matthew, where Joseph is the central figure receiving the angelic revelation while Mary is taking on a more passive role, it is Mary who receives the angelic visitation and accepts God's plan in Luke: "I am the Lord's servant, may it be as you have said" (1:38). It is from this moment, celebrated in Christian liturgy as the Feast of the Annunciation (March 25), that Mary assumes the title of the Virgin. After the annunciation, Mary spends three months with her cousin Elizabeth and never consults Joseph through any of these events, according to Luke. She is the central player in Jesus' birth, although Joseph is at her side. Clearly, it is the Mary of Luke's narrative that would become the source of Marian theology.

Yet the problem of Mary's virginity is, in fact, quite complex and multi—faceted. Countless theological debates raged throughout the centuries until the problem was eventually resolved in the mid—nineteenth century. These debates were partly a result of the fact that the Christian scriptures do not indicate whether Mary remained a virgin *after* the birth of Jesus. Christian authors until the Reformation upheld the belief that she was *ever virgin*: before, after, and even during the birth of her son. This belief is referred to as "perpetual virginity." The idea that Mary and Joseph lived together as a regular married couple after the birth of Jesus, who had several brothers and sisters, was emphatically rejected by the early Church tradition. The developing asceticism of the early Christian movement considered virginity to be the purest state, while sexual relations in marriage were viewed as "less pure." Not surprisingly, this belief made all assumptions that the brothers and sisters of Jesus were equally Mary's biological children unacceptable. Hence, Mary's subsequent sexual relations with Joseph and her maternity of Jesus' brothers and sisters had to be denied. This idea was later revived during the Reformation and remains the modern Protestant belief about Mary.

Mary's authority and her significance in Eastern Orthodoxy and Roman Catholicism are rooted in her obedience to God's plan and in her free consent to give birth to Jesus Christ, God incarnate. At the Council of Ephesus in 431 CE, Mary was officially proclaimed *theotokos*, which means "god—bearer." It is probably no coincidence that this proclamation occurred in Ephesus (modern—day Turkey), for this was the same place in which the great temple dedicated to the Greek goddess Artemis stood for centuries – until her cult was prohibited by the Christian emperor Theodosius in 380 CE. The people of Ephesus, deprived of their goddess, readily turned to Mary. Yet the title *Theotokos* in relation to Mary – which redefined her position in response to popular demand – had also been the subject of a major controversy that erupted in the Eastern Church prior to the council at Ephesus. This controversy was related to the definition of the two natures of Jesus Christ, divine and human. Two major questions arose: Were Jesus' two natures separate, so that Mary could be spoken of only as mother of his human nature? Or were the two natures rather so commingled that she could be spoken of as Godbearer? The two natures of Christ were eventually defined as both distinct and whole in and of themselves – and, at the same time, as united. The argument that the incarnation of Christ brought together the two natures into one divine—human union, thus ending any separation, made it ultimately possible and even appropriate to speak of Mary as *Theotokos*. However, this title is not to be misunderstood in the sense of Mary being literally God's mother. In bearing Christ's humanity, Mary also bore one who was God.

Although this title allowed Christians to venerate Mary as one who had borne God, controversy remained about the status of her own conception and death. This particular problem, which would not be fully resolved until the mid—nineteenth century, was related to the Christian belief that humans had originally been created with sinless bodies that were not subject to death. Yet disobedience caused them to "fall" into mortal bodies, which then, in turn, necessitated sexual reproduction. If Mary *herself* had been conceived sexually, presumably she shared in this same sinful mortality. Similar to the

controversial issue of perpetual virginity, the problem
of Mary's sinlessness continued to be debated among
theologians for centuries. Eventually, the idea of Mary's
particular status was extended based on the account of
her miraculous birth in the Proevangelium of James. This
text, which fills in the blanks of the biblical accounts
on Mary's birth, tells of an angelic appearance to Anna,
Mary's aged mother, announcing to her that her child
would be dedicated to the service of God (echoing the later
story of the Annunciation to Mary). Although Mary was
not regarded as having been conceived by the Holy Spirit,
as was the case with Jesus Christ, her human conception
was nevertheless perceived as marked by a special divine
grace. This grace sanctified her in Anna's womb, thus
freeing her from the original sin with which all other
humans are marked.

While it is ultimately impossible to know what happened
literally on the physical plane, the motif of virgin birth
is a powerful metaphor of purity that appears not only in
the Christian tradition but also across the world cultures,
such as in the legends surrounding the historical Buddha
Shakyamuni's birth. In fact, belief in impregnation of
a mortal woman by a god belongs to most traditions in
the pre—Christian world. The Greek god Dionysus, for
example, was born of a virgin Semele who wished to see
the supreme "Sky—Father" Zeus in all his divine glory
and was mysteriously impregnated by one of his bolts
of lightning. The theme of Mary's virgin birth likely has
roots in the tradition of the pagan "Virgin Goddesses."
In the Greco—Roman world, many goddesses were called
virgins. This did not imply that chastity was considered
a virtue in the pre—Christian world. Rather, Greek
goddesses such as Artemis or Athena were embodiments
of a virginity that symbolized autonomy, independence,
and the freedom to take lovers or to reject them. In this

context, the term "virgin" differs considerably from the common Christian understanding. It implies that the pagan goddesses were *true* to their *intrinsic nature*, sufficient onto themselves in the act of conception and birth, *not* maiden inviolate. In this context, we may also note the pioneering work of scholar and author Marguerite Rigoglioso, whose primary focus of research are the "Virgin Mothers" of the ancient Mediterranean world. In *The Cult of the Divine Births in Ancient Greece* and *Virgin Mother Goddesses of Antiquity*, Rigoglioso reminds us that some of these pre—Christian "Virgin Mothers" – the Greek goddesses Artemis, Athena, Hera, Demeter and Persephone – possessed the highly advanced esoteric skills necessary to produce life *from within themselves without a male consort.* Self—generative virgin goddesses were viewed as "primordial creatrix" who required no male partner to produce the cosmos, earth, and all of life.

Yet in Hellenistic dualistic thinking – historians refer to the age of Alexander the Great (356—323 BCE) and his successors as the Hellenistic age when Greek cultural traditions spread far beyond *hellas,* that is, Greece – body and spirit increasingly came to be viewed as separate. Female sexuality was identified with the body and feared. The early Christian church fathers adopted this concept, afraid that reason would be overthrown by passion. Spiritual fulfillment was sought through detachment from earthly concerns and bodily pleasures.

In their ascetic revolt, the early Christians hence needed to exempt the Mother of Christ from tainted sexuality in order to proclaim her purity and perpetual virginity. From a theological point of view, it was the immaculate womb of the Virgin that made redemption possible. The second century CE saw the first major emergence of Mary's redemptive role based on Luke's infancy narrative.

In addition, drawing on Paul's theme of Christ as the new Adam, several second—century church fathers created a parallel role for Mary as the new Eve. Mary's pure womb helped to overcome the sin of the first Eve. Through her faithfulness and obedience, Mary became the new Eve. Yet the notion of Mary as the second Eve comes with an ambiguous and problematic legacy. In an odd inversion, Mary as the new Eve is sometimes pictured in Christian iconography as trampling the snake/dragon, the ancient guardian of the shrines of Mother Earth and a characteristic symbol of the powerful pre—Christian goddesses since the prehistoric period. In the Christian tradition, the serpent is viewed in an uncommonly negative light. Through her obedience, Mary as the new Eve facilitates the birth of the Son of God, through whom death and the serpent are destroyed. Mary's redemptive obedience hence precedes and makes possible Jesus' redemptive work.

By the Middle Ages, a feast dedicated to Mary's Immaculate Conception was already celebrated annually on December 8, although medieval theologians continued to debate the problem of Mary's exemption from original sin. In 1854, the Immaculate Conception was finally proclaimed to be the official doctrine by Pope Pius IX in response to an immensely popular demand that had its roots in the twelfth century CE. Mary was now officially defined as completely cleansed from the effects of original sin in the very act of being conceived and, in addition, as having conceived immaculately. As "ever—virgin," Mary's uncorrupt womb would set her apart from all the other women, who, as "daughters of the first Eve," gave physical birth through "corrupt" wombs which were tainted by original sin. In Mary, and in her alone, the virginal consecration was combined with the tremendous dignity of human motherhood. Mary's life was declared to be completely without blemish. She was the only human who was considered free of the will to sin. In fact, Mary was now regarded as the most perfect being after Jesus Christ, conceived in all purity by the creator. And yet, all this glory of Mary as reflected in Christian iconography "cannot undo the misogyny of Christian theology in which human sexuality and women's bodies are considered evil,"[19] as Elinor Gadon puts it.

The Assumption

The Assumption of the Virgin Mary

Mary's status was even more elevated in 1950, when the doctrine of the Assumption was officially proclaimed by Pope Pius XII. His announcement that Mary had been taken up body and soul into the glory of heaven was greeted with tears of joy, thunderous clapping, and resonant prayers. Since then, Mary's death and resurrection are officially celebrated on August 15. The proclamation of Mary's bodily assumption as an article of faith only made official a long—standing belief. In fact, since the early seventh century CE, Mary's Dormition (which means

---

[19] Gadon, *The Once and Future Goddess*, p. 208.

"falling asleep" in death) had already been celebrated on the fifteenth of August.

Yet what do we really know about the circumstances of Mary's death? The New Testament does not supply specific details. The place of her death has not (yet) been determined, and no tomb or bodily remains of the Virgin have ever been found. Speculation abounds, however, about Jerusalem and Ephesus as likely places of her death. Texts known as Mary's Dormition, that are equally part of the pseudepigraphical tradition, provide us with the following description of Mary's last day to fill in some of the blanks of the biblical accounts. After Jesus' death Mary was visited by an angel, eventually receiving reassurance that she would soon be reunited with her son. Shortly thereafter, Mary died surrounded by the apostles. As her body was placed in the tomb, Jesus Christ appeared in a cloud of light surrounded by angels. Mary's soul came to be reunited with her body in the process of ascending. As was the case of Mary's birth, her death was described in terms that were clearly reminiscent of Jesus Christ's own ascension.

Eastern and Western Christians basically agreed that, as a result of Mary's virginal purity, her body did not suffer common corruption at death. Yet the question of whether her body was preserved in some paradise to be united with her soul at the general resurrection, or whether she had been resurrected and ascended bodily into heaven immediately after her death, remained open until the issue was eventually resolved in 1950 with the official proclamation of her bodily assumption. Mary, the virginal mother and epitome of Christian virtue, had now been installed in heaven side—by—side with Christ to provide assistance to all her distressed supplicants.

Another fundamental question arises: Did the Assumption imply that Mary was now considered on par with the Holy Trinity? Christian theology testifies to one God in three persons: Father, Son, and Holy Spirit. Insofar as these three persons are understood anthropomorphically, as in the visual arts, they are portrayed as male. Although the Church officially acknowledges Mary's purity and her co—redemptive role as *Theotokos*, she is clearly *not* considered on par with the Trinity from a theological standpoint. Officially, Mary is chosen to bear divinity as a maiden who is untainted by the "stain" of sexual relations. But she is *not divine in her own right.* The special position she holds between the divine and human realms is most accurately expressed by the degree of her worship as officially sanctioned by the church. For example, God is owed adoration, while the saints may receive veneration. For Mary as the most prominent of the Christian saints "superior veneration" is deemed appropriate. In many areas, however, Mary is and has been worshiped as devoutly and fervently as the ancient pre—Christian goddesses. From a theological perspective one could argue that the whole of life cannot be experienced through her because she is set apart from the laws of nature by which humanity is bound, most notably with regard to the absence of the sacred dimension of sexuality. Mary is exalted yet at the same time she is denied both the status of a goddess and the complete humanity of a woman. Moreover, Mary does *not* bring forth the world from the inexhaustible source within her womb, as was the case with the "Mother Goddess" of the prehistoric period.

Even so, the doctrine of Assumption clearly elevated Mary's status. Christians now had a "Mother in Heaven" to whom they could turn when the archetypal "Father God" and his Son appeared impervious to their needs. The Assumption of Mary "ratified her uncorrupted goodness and so held out to believers the hope that they too could look for such an eventual unification of redeemed soul and uncorrupted body in a heavenly world to come."[20] Nowhere is the power of the Virgin more graphically expressed than in the *Vierge Ouvrante*, a small French votive sculpture from the thirteenth century that illustrates the popular yet heterodox belief that without her, redemption would not have been possible. When the sculpture is closed, the Virgin offering a small globe or fruit to her child is on display. When opened, we see the entire Trinity – Father, Son, and Holy Spirit – contained within her body. This thirteenth—century representation of the Virgin is one of the most striking examples in Christian iconography of Mary as the great "Divine Mother" whose womb brings forth the entire universe. This particular sculpture also relates Mary to the tradition of the great Goddess figures of pre—Christian cultures and the tantric religions of the East.

Mary as the "Queen of Heaven"

Only four years after declaring the Assumption official doctrine, the Roman Catholic Church proclaimed Mary "Queen of Heaven" in 1954. Notably, Mary was not declared "Queen of the Earth." From the viewpoint of Christian theology, this is not surprising since nature had come to be regarded as "fallen" and apart from the divine. Heaven and Earth were increasingly viewed in terms of incompatible polarities.

The proclamation of Mary as "Queen of Heaven" was, in fact, the culmination of a long tradition of Christian iconography dating from the medieval period.

---

[20] Radford Ruether, *Goddesses and the Divine Feminine*, p. 164.

In a rendering by the Italian artist Agnolo Gaddi (c.1370) of the coronation of Mary, Christ places the crown reverently upon his mother's head. This contrasts the mythic narratives surrounding pre—Christian goddesses: it is here the son who places the crown on his mother's head, *not* the mother—goddess endorsing the rule of her pharaoh—son and installing him on her throne as was, for example, the case with Isis in Egypt.

Mary had already appeared crowned as the "Queen of Heaven" in the portals of some of the great medieval cathedrals such as Chartres and Notre Dame of Paris. Yet her image as "Queen of Heaven" is somewhat ambiguous in that it reflects both her intrinsic power *and* the political ambitions of the Roman Catholic Church. Particularly in her regal representations, Mary appears to be an embodiment of the Church's universal aspirations. In sculpture and wall paintings, mosaic and stained glass, she is enthroned as empress with the symbols of universal power. Mary was at times co—opted with the purpose of serving as a potent symbol of the alliance between politics and institutionalized religion. Her emblem was, for example, pinned to the standards of Christian armies throughout history. Military victories were often attributed to the Virgin's intervention similar to instances in which some of the pre—Christian goddesses were affiliated with warfare and military success, most notably Inanna and Athena. In this particular function, Mary assumes the broader role of guarantor of the "divine order" as it was believed to be reflected in the authority of the imperial Church and in the hierarchical structures of medieval society on the "earthly" plane. Sheltering the Christian people with her cloak, Mary ultimately also came to symbolize the protective powers represented by "Mother Church." These are but a few examples that reveal how goddess figures and symbols of the Divine

Feminine are adopted to reflect patriarchal paradigms and values systems.

During the medieval period, the great devotional hymns *Salve Regina* and *Regina Caeli* were composed in honor of Mary's particular function as the exalted "Queen of Heaven." Interestingly, this honorific title predates the Christian tradition, appearing already in inscriptions and hymns from the second millennium BCE that were dedicated to prominent goddesses such as Inanna/Ishtar and Isis. As the "Great Lady of Heaven," these pre—Christian goddesses were personified in the morning stars Sirius and Venus. In Egypt, Isis was identified with the bright star Sirius (Sothis) that would rise at the time when the Nile was about to flood the parched lands. Similarly, some representations show Mary with stars circling her head like a halo of light. Mary with a crown of stars is an image that is also evocative of Inanna/ Ishtar, who, as a moon goddess, wore as her crown the twelve constellations through which the sun moved. The iconography of Mary's relation to the stars, the moon, and the sun takes its ostensible reference from the passage in the Book of Revelation (12:1) where she is depicted as being clothed with the radiance of the sun, the moon under her feet, and a crown of twelve stars upon her head (we may note, though, that interpretations of this female celestial figure in Revelation vary). The moon has equally been a symbol of the great Goddess since Paleolithic times. Like some of the lunar goddesses predating her, Mary is the mistress of the rhythmic ebb and flow of the waters and the menstrual cycle. Many pre—Christian goddesses such as Isis and Aphrodite were said to emerge from the waters. The Virgin's name, Maria, is etymologically related to the Latin term *mare*, which means the sea. Mary's blue robe also represents the color of the sea and the skies.

Mary eventually became the patroness of ships and sailors, which amounted to a life—saving function during an age in which maritime navigation was primarily guided by the stars. Mary may have inherited her title "Star of the Sea" from Isis. In this context, we may note that in ancient Egypt the heavens were conceived as an integral part of the primordial waters. Not surprisingly, ancient Egyptian goddesses were referred to as the "watery abyss of heaven." For example Hathor, the great "cow of heaven" later equated with Isis, was praised for sustaining her people with her milk that would fall as the fertilizing rain. Mary's function as the "Heavenly Mother" concerned with fertility and childbirth evokes a similar image.

During the medieval period, women in particular sought the comfort and solace of Mary's presence at times of pregnancy and childbirth. Agricultural people in particular celebrated the seasonal festivals invoking Mary's gifts of abundance and fertility. The Virgin nursing the Christ child is referred to as *dea nutrix* in Latin. Mary's capacity to nurture is, next to her immaculate womb, one of her most prominent features. In fact, the miraculous powers of her breast milk have been praised since the medieval period when her pilgrimage route in Western Europe was also known as the "Milky Way." In Renaissance art, Mary is sometimes portrayed as the nursing mother of the Christian saints as well. Numerous healings attested to her tell how the Virgin sprinkled sweet milk over her supplicants, thereby curing them miraculously with her powers. Similar to Mary, the Chinese "Goddess of Compassion" Kuan Shi Yin in Mahayana Buddhism is also known for healing the sick and assisting women in childbirth. In an iconographic resemblance to Mary, Kuan Yin sometimes carries a child on her arm. To her female supplicants, she symbolizes the ability to give them children endowed with numerous perfections of mind and body.

Mary's assistance in childbirth as well as her healing and nursing functions are but one of the many paradoxes she embodies within the framework of Christian theology. The new faith was unable to ignore the potent symbols, namely, the womb and the breasts, of women's "earthly" bodies. Yet problems of Mary's human incarnation continued to plague theologians, leading to convoluted reasoning in an effort to establish a doctrine that would accommodate both popular Marian devotion and the Church's view of the new "divine order."

Aside from the doctrinal considerations of the imperial Church, the mother of Christ had been revered as the "Queen of Heaven" and the mediator between the human and divine realms since the Middle Ages. This devotion reflected a profound desire in the collective psyche of Western civilization to include an archetypal image of the feminine in its conception of the divine. Mary was considered the most accessible of those standing in the presence of God, and it was believed that prayers to her would be passed along with a strong recommendation. Mary soon became the guarantor of human hopes and yearnings, as another of her numerous titles, "Wide—Open Gate of Heaven," attests. The latter is related to Mary's function as the merciful and powerful intercessor with her son for the souls of the deceased. This function is exemplified most prominently in the closing plea of the "Hail Mary," prayed across the Catholic world: "Pray for us sinners, now and at the hour of our death." In her role as the intercessor for the souls of the dead, Mary is, once again, symbolically and thematically related to pre—Christian goddesses such as Inanna who voluntarily embarks on a journey to the underworld with the purpose of receiving initiation into the mysteries of death.

Finally, Mary's affiliation with death is apparent in her other function as the "Mother Dolorosa," namely, the sorrowful mother who has been given an immortal testament in Michelangelo's Pieta in Saint Peter's Basilica. In this sculpture, Mary's profound grief at the death of her son assumes the broader dimension of universal human loss. The underlying message of this masterpiece is that the Virgin understands our sorrows as humans and assists us in our suffering. More fundamentally, she fully shares in her son's agony, standing at the cross and offering his suffering to the divine as a sacrifice for the redemption of the world. Her lament echoes the grief of all pre—Christian goddesses for their son—lovers and/or their children. This scenario is seen in the lament of Inanna for Dumuzi, Isis for Osiris, and, finally, Demeter for her daughter Persephone. Like the pagan lunar goddesses, Mary is metaphorically affiliated with the dark moon in her function as the guardian of the mysteries of death and transformation. She mourns the loss of her son during the three days between his crucifixion and his resurrection. These are also the three days of darkness when the moon disappears before the dormant light of the crescent is eventually reawakened.

The Black Madonna (Lithuania-Vilna)

The Black Virgin

Since the tenth century CE, the shrines of the Black
Virgin were the most venerated in Europe. Her sacred
sites attracted, and still continue to attract, crowds of
devotees beseeching her favors. Black icons of the Virgin
were commonly believed to be more powerful than the
white versions. Miraculous cures proliferated at the
shrines of Black Madonnas. Some of her statues, clothed
in magnificent robes and jewels, marked the stages on
the great pilgrimage route to Santiago de Compostela in
northern Spain. Black Madonnas can also be found in
France, Poland, Italy, Switzerland, Germany, Russia and
elsewhere. Often, the cult sites honoring pre—Christian
goddesses were rededicated to the Virgin to allow the
people to continue their devotion to an archetypal image

of the Divine Feminine. For example, a temple of Isis was found underneath the cathedral of the Black Virgin at Le Puy in France. In *Dark Mother*, feminist scholar Lucia Chiavola Birnbaum argues that images of Black Madonnas may be our most palpable evidence of the persisting memory of the primordial dark mother of Africa on the white continent of Europe. Birnbaum, who has literally researched hundreds of Black Virgins across Europe, has mainly come to this conclusion based on her observations that some of the dark icons of the Virgin, most prominently those in France, are reminiscent of lean and tall African sculptures. Examples are La Vierge Noire de Saint Gervazy in Puy de Dome, La Vierge de Sous—Terre de Chartres, and a statue of the Virgin referred to as La Negrette in Espalion. Notre Dame de Meymac, also called "the Egyptian," even has a turban on her head. In this context, we may note that many pre—Christian goddesses such as Isis, Demeter, Athena, and Artemis of Ephesus had black representations as well. In the famous *Song of Songs*, the Shulamite woman declared that she was black, and the Hindu goddess Kali is strikingly dark as well. Indeed, black female deities can be found on all continents, a fact that is likely related to African migrations to the other continents during the prehistoric period.

With European Black Madonnas originating most likely in prehistoric Africa, the question arises: What about the deeper significance and the symbolism of the color 'black' that characterizes so many cross—cultural representations of the Divine Feminine? Perhaps the Virgin is black because she is also an embodiment of the ancient Earth Mother. This makes sense when considering that the deeper layers of the earth are not only darker but are also the most fertile. Perhaps this is one reason why the worship of the Black Virgin has been particularly popular among peasants since the Middle Ages. Despite strong opposition by the established Church during the medieval period, this devotion has persisted into the present. As the Dark Mother, Mary is an embodiment of all the elemental forces of nature, symbolizing the earth and the waters. In creation mythology across the world's cultures, darkness is indeed at the beginning. The Dark Mother is thus, to a certain extent, the original mother.

Black Virgins renowned for their healing powers are often affiliated with wooded areas, lakes, rivers, grottoes, and caves, as well as with the subterranean and volcanic earth. Birnbaum reminds us of the connection between black rocks and sacred sites dedicated to the Dark Mother. In her particular function as the earth, the Black Virgin also assumes the role of mother to the animals. In fact, in some Renaissance paintings, Mary is found sitting on a lion throne, which places her in the long tradition of pre—Christian goddesses embodying the powers of raw nature. Examples include the Minoan "Goddess of the Animals" who stands on top of a mountain flanked by lions, and other "Goddesses of the Beasts" such as Artemis to whom wild animals are sacred.

The Dark Mother may also be a metaphor of the night, death, and the mysteries that Western culture has collectively repressed for centuries regarding female sexuality and the fear of death. In the traditions of monotheistic orthodoxy, the color "black" has come to signify "impurity" and "evil" – as opposed to the mystical—esoteric traditions within Judaism, Christianity, and Islam, which provide more positive connotations for the color. One of the features of Goddess religion is the positive interpretation and valuation of "blackness" and "darkness." Hence, the image of the Black Virgin, as well as other dark representations of the Divine Feminine, call on us to transcend any conditioned socio—cultural patterns of understanding "light" and "darkness" that are entrenched in our collective consciousness. The Black Virgin symbolizes the fathomless mystery of the soul, which must embark on its arduous night journey before eventually attaining a deeper understanding of the true meaning of life *and* death. Standing upon altars of remote chapels and on underground crypts of cathedrals, the image of the Dark Mother relates to both the dark earthly womb of gestation and the realm of the dark moon, that is, the creative depths from which the old light has vanished but the new light will be reborn.

Similar to the lunar Hindu goddess Kali, Black Madonnas are venerated for both their regenerative and their destructive powers. The Dark Mother represents the shattering of the old paradigms that precede transformation. The dark phase of the lunar cycle is where light gestates to be transformed and brought forth anew. Darkness may thus be viewed as a metaphor for wisdom. As Cashford and Baring remind us, the statues of the Black Virgin equally symbolize Sophia—Sapientia, the personification of the ancient biblical Wisdom tradition that had to be studied and taught in the utmost secrecy under fear of torture and death by fire because it threatened the official Church doctrine. As a catalyst for alchemical transformation, the Dark Mother sustains the work of repair and healing of the world. But healing can only occur on the basis of social justice. Consequently, Black Madonnas are often affiliated with the oppressed and disenfranchised. An example is the Virgin of Guadalupe, patron saint of the Americas, who sustains Mexican farm workers in their liberation struggle for social justice.

Images of the Black Virgin have evolved in Latin America with the blending of Catholicism with Native American deities on the one hand and African cults on the other. Most notably, the veneration of the Virgin of Guadalupe represents a syncretism of the Catholic Mary with the pre—Columbian mother goddess Tonantzin. In fact, a pilgrimage shrine dedicated to the earth goddess Tonantzin previously existed at the same site in pre—Hispanic times. To this day, some Mexican Indians continue to refer to the Virgin by her Mexican name. Mary appeared at the site of Tonantzin's shrine only ten years after the Spanish conquest. The narrative of the apparition served as a symbolic testimony to the Indians that their goddess was still alive. Yet the Virgin of Guadalupe conveys a somewhat ambiguous symbolic message. Rosemary Radford—Ruether comments: "Guadalupe, as the 'Goddess of the Americas,' has been and continues to be today a multivalent symbol that can both validate reactionary trends of the patriarchal Mexican church and society and nonetheless be endlessly reappropriated and interpreted from revolutionary, liberative, and feminist perspectives."[21]

The Black Virgin remains a powerful symbol in Latin America for social justice and for the recognition that all people are ultimately one. In Italy, the Black Madonna, in her role as the protectress of the disenfranchised, is represented in the strikingly dark Madonna del Popolo, which means "Mother of the People," found in the Brancacci Chapel in Florence. In Rome, seat of the papacy, the Madonna del Popolo in Santa Maria Maggiore has been whitened, according to Lucia Chiavola—Birnbaum. She has also made another interesting observation as related to the black virgins of France. Most of the infants held by the French dark mothers are *not* infants at all, but rather miniature adults who seem to be conveying

---

[21] Radford Ruether, *Goddesses and the Divine Feminine*, p. 9.

the universal message that the Black Mother embraces *all* people, no matter what their gender, sexual orientation, social status, or religious and political affiliation. In our modern and postmodern times, the Dark Mother may well be the carrier of the new transformative consciousness that has the power to shift the global collective field of consciousness and is, in fact, already shifting it at the time of this writing. Finally, in popular understanding, Black Madonnas are related to Mary Magdalene, a figure that has been equally subversive of Church doctrine.

Giacomo Galli, The Penitent Mary Magdalene
(1620 to 1640)

MARY MAGDALENE: FORGOTTEN BRIDE OF CHRISTIANITY?

F ew figures in Christian literature are as provocative, controversial, and mysterious as Mary Magdalene, the "apostle to the apostles," who was Jesus' most beloved disciple according to some apocryphal or noncanonical texts. For millennia, she has challenged Christian notions of sexuality, gender, and spiritual embodiment. In *The Resurrection of Mary Magdalene*, scholar Jane Schaberg writes: "The volatile figure of Mary Magdalene is so far too big for Hollywood, which sees her as a mix of lust, loyalty, belief, prostitution, repentance, beauty, madness, sainthood. She is the strange woman, silent, dominated by the great image of Jesus crucified, resurrected. She symbolizes the belief that women are made only deficiently in the image of God, and are ultimately a symbol of...dependent, sinful humanity. But women can be forgiven; eros can be controlled. Male fantasies about the Magdalene have fired the imagination of artists, made her an instrument of ecclesiastical propaganda, and misshaped lives."[22]

Apart from the numerous fantasies, projections, and controversies that erupted around the figure of Mary Magdalene, the earliest Christian literature generally portrays her as a prominent disciple of Jesus, as attested to by the frequent practice of placing her name first in the lists of women followers. Sadly, Mary Magdalene is usually thought of as a broken person whose conversion was synonymous with her healing. Even the contemporary liturgical prayers for the Feast of Mary Magdalene (July 22) maintain this emphasis on healing and restitution. But what do we know about Mary Magdalene? How is she portrayed in both the canonical and the noncanonical Gospels? And what can be said about the nature of her relationship to Jesus Christ in the light of recent research?

Mary Magdalene in the Canonical Gospels and in Traditional Christianity

The canonical Gospels tell us little about the life of the historical Mary Magdalene. Scholars commonly assume that the epithet "Magdalene" indicates that she came from the town of Magdala (Migdal), located on the west shore of the Sea of Galilee just north of the city of Tiberias. However, in *Mary Magdalene, Bride in Exile*,

---

[22] Schaberg, *The Resurrection of Mary Magdalene*, p. 8.

Margaret Starbird argues that the title Magdalene is an honorific given to her, reflecting her preeminent status among the earliest Christians. Along with other women, Mary Magdalene accompanied Jesus of Nazareth throughout his ministry. All four Gospels either directly mention or allude to the fact that Mary Magdalene is present at the crucifixion and burial. Her presence at the garden tomb provides irrefutable grounds for her elevated status as an apostle. Interestingly, all four Gospels state that Mary Magdalene stands firm when all the other disciples are fleeing because they are haunted by fears of being arrested. She does not run, and she does not betray or lie about her commitment. Mary's steadfast character and her unwavering attitude in the face of acute danger and distress is an unmistakable demonstration of either the most profound human love or the highest spiritual understanding of what Jesus was teaching, perhaps both.

Remarkably, all four canonical Gospels also identify Mary Magdalene as having been the *first witness* to Jesus' resurrection, and they all single her out individually for this particular role. While the details vary, and the jury is split as to whether Mary Magdalene appeared alone or in a group of other women, all four Gospels mention her *by name* as the first witness to the resurrection. The fact that Mary Magdalene is given unparalleled distinction as the preeminent witness to the resurrection of Jesus in all four versions of the story officially accepted as historical is indeed highly significant. Moreover, all four Gospels portray her in the role of "apostle to the apostles," that is, as the first to announce the good news of the resurrection publicly. It is in the Gospel of John (20:17—18) that the risen Jesus gives her special teachings and commissions her to announce the good news of his resurrection to the other disciples. In John, Jesus gently but firmly reminds the ecstatic Mary Magdalene that his return to human flesh will be brief, and he instructs her not "to cling" to him. Love always exists in the eternity of their hearts, yet the time for clinging is over and the time for proclamation has begun.

Unlike Mary Magdalene's role in the Passion and resurrection narratives attested to in all four canonical Gospels, the report of her former demonic possession comes only through Luke (8:2), the only independent source to communicate this. Within the context of the times, "being possessed by demons" could imply either an emotional or recurrent physical illness. In modern terms, Mary Magdalene may have done "psychological shadow work" to cleanse herself. No mention of any infirmity is in Matthew, John, or any of the noncanonical Gospels. Even Luke does *not* say anything about the "seven demons" of Mary Magdalene that is in any way related to prostitution, nor does he call Mary a "sinner." In addition, Luke (8:3) is the only one to mention that Mary Magdalene was of independent means and supported Jesus out of her own resources. If this level of support is a historical fact, it would indicate that certain women had significant resources at their disposal and, more particularly, that Mary was indeed Jesus' patron. Scholars have been skeptical about these two bits of data. One reason is that this information is given only in Luke, the other that the comment on Mary's demonic possession fits into Luke's overall tendency to undercut Mary Magdalene's credibility as the premiere witness to the resurrection and to reduce her status, especially in comparison with the enhanced roles of Peter and the twelve male apostles. In any case, it is safe to say that Luke's account planted the first seeds of doubt about Mary Magdalene's character. Even though she had been healed, the story of Mary's possession portrays her as unclean and susceptible to demonic influence. And, as we shall see, these seeds continued to grow. Luke's brief comment on the healing of Mary Magdalene's mysterious "illness of mind or body" would soon become the chief feature of her portrait in the Christian West. But to understand how Mary Magdalene became the "repentant whore," we first need to examine another episode reported in all four canonical Gospels.

In a highly dramatic incident that takes place while Jesus is at dinner with friends, an unnamed woman bursts into the dining room carrying a jar of precious perfume. She opens it and copiously anoints Jesus' head or feet, weeping all the while. The host attempts to protest her behavior but Jesus staunchly defends her actions. While all four Gospels are unanimous in their testimony that this incident happened, the actual portrayal of the unnamed woman and the timing vary widely. Matthew, Mark, and John set the episode directly before the crucifixion. In this context, the incident assumes the meaning of a burial anointment, as also attested to by Jesus himself. Interestingly enough, Luke's account (7:36—50) is the only one that separates this episode from the Holy Week narrative and places it within the context of Jesus' public ministry where it loses its expressly symbolic and ceremonial references. Further, Luke uniquely introduces the unnamed woman as a "sinner." He fills in the details, painting the picture of an effusive emotionality by mentioning tears, weeping, and kissing of feet. Luke also adds a comment by Simon the Pharisee about "what kind of a woman this was," which implies that her "sin" must be lust (read: prostitution). Finally, he comments on the fact that Jesus forgives this woman because she "loves much," a statement that can of course be read as referring to the large number of her sexual relationships rather than that she has just performed a loving act. Luke, however, does *not* identify this anointing woman as Mary Magdalene – and neither do John, Matthew, and Mark. John calls this woman Mary of Bethany, referring to Lazarus' sister.

So how did we get this picture of Mary Magdalene as the "repentant whore?" By putting the pieces together, merging Luke's details with the composite portrait emerging from the other three Gospels, a story started to take shape. In the fourth century, Christian theologians in the Latin West began to associate Mary Magdalene (from whom "seven demons were casted out") with the "unnamed sinner," who anointed Jesus' feet in Luke. Further confusion resulted by conflating the account of John, in which Mary of Bethany anoints Jesus, with the unnamed woman in Luke's account. At the end of the sixth century, Pope Gregory the Great gave a sermon in which he not only identified these figures, but also drew the moral conclusion that would dominate the imagination of the West for centuries to come:

> *She whom Luke calls the sinful woman, whom John calls Mary, we believe to be the Mary from whom seven devils were ejected...And what did these seven devils signify, if not all the vices?...It is clear, brothers, that the woman previously used the unguent to perfume her flesh in forbidden acts. What she therefore displayed more scandalously, she was now offering to God in a more praiseworthy manner. She had coveted with earthly eyes, but now through penitence these are consumed with tears... She turned the mass of her crimes to virtues, in order to serve God entirely in penance, for as much as she had wrongly held God in contempt.* [23]

---

[23] Quoted from Karen King, *The Gospel of Mary of Magdala*, p. 151.

Once these initial identifications were in place, Mary Magdalene could be associated with every unnamed sinful woman in the Gospels, including the adulteress in John (8:1—11) and the Syro—Phoenician woman with her five and more "husbands" in John (4:7—30). Mary the apostle and teacher was transformed into a "repentant whore." This portrait defined the Roman Catholic Church's official position on Mary Magdalene for nearly fourteen hundred years until 1969 when the teaching that she was a prostitute was finally repealed. The image of Mary as a prostitute and adulteress explained why she was unworthy to touch Jesus' resurrected body, and reinforced the view that women were to be perceived in terms of their sexuality, rather than as beings with significant spiritual potential. For the church fathers, "this fiction solved two problems at once by undermining both the teachings associated with Mary and women's capacity to take on leadership roles,"[24] according to feminist scholar Karen King. Women could be defined based on their sexual roles and their relations to men – as virgins, wives, mothers, widows, or prostitutes. Nowhere are these stereotypical notions and perceptions more apparent than in the polarized view of the virtuous and chaste Mother Mary on the one hand, and the "penitent sinner" Mary Magdalene on the other. It almost appears as if the need for one extreme created the need for the other. But these models of female behavior are problematic. They lead to prejudice and severely inhibit women from experiencing themselves as fully integrated human beings. Both virgin and whore are terms for different kinds of sexual service.

Additional aspects further explain why Mary Magdalene became the "penitent whore." In her insightful book, *The Meaning of Mary Magdalene*, Cynthia Bourgeault

---

[24] King, *The Gospel of Mary of Magdala*, p. 152.

concludes that this portrait of Mary Magdalene is the work of the early church's collective unconsciousness, the inevitable shadow side of its increasing obsession with celibacy and sexual purity. Moreover, the image of Mary as the "redeemed sinner" has nourished an empathy that deeply resonates with our human imperfection, frailty, and mortality. From a psychological perspective, a fallen redeemer figure holds out the hope that purity and wholeness are never closed off and that redemption is always a possibility at hand. Despite the appropriation of sinful female sexuality for patriarchal purposes, Mary Magdalene's rich legacy in Christian art and literature clearly attests to the redemptive power of the "repentant sinner."

Mary Magdalene's Portrait in the Noncanonical Gospels of Early Christianity

Early Christian literature, recently discovered in Egypt, has enhanced our knowledge of how Mary was perceived in the first centuries of Christian belief. The most significant sources are the Gospel of Mary (Magdalene), four tightly written dialogues that were found in 1896 and deliver powerful new revelations on the nature of Jesus' teachings; and the so—called Nag Hammadi collection that was recovered in 1945. The latter texts include, among others, the Gospel of Thomas and the Gospel of Philip. While the canonical Gospels place an emphasis on "right belief" as the precondition for salvation, the Gospels of Mary Magdalene, Thomas, and Philip belong to the wider tradition of universal wisdom with its core notion of "right practice" – that is, experiential and direct illumination that eventually leads to profound inner transformation.

What these noncanonical scriptures all have in common is that they portray Mary Magdalene as one of the interlocutors in dialogues of Jesus with his disciples. Mary is an active and vocal participant. She speaks frequently and acts as a representative of the disciples as a group, addressing several questions to Jesus. She is included among those special disciples to whom Jesus entrusts his most elevated teaching. In fact, Mary is frequently praised for her profound insight. For example, in the Dialogue of the Savior, a second—century writing, Mary Magdalene appears as a prominent disciple and the only woman named. In response to a particularly insightful question asked by Mary, Jesus says to her: "You show the abundance of the one who reveals" (DSav 140:17—19). And at another point after Mary has spoken, the narrator confirms that she uttered these words "as a woman who understood everything" (DSav 139:11—13).

Other noncanonical texts use the figure of Mary Magdalene to suggest that women's activity challenged the leaders of the orthodox Christian community, who regarded the apostle Peter as their spokesman. In the third—century text Pistis Sophia ("Faith Wisdom"), Mary Magdalene again appears to be preeminent among the disciples, taking the lead in asking questions. Peter, who is portrayed as a jealous, misogynist disciple, complains that Mary is dominating the conversation with Jesus and is hence undermining the rightful priority of him and his brother apostles. He urges Jesus to silence her and is quickly rebuked. Jesus replies that whoever is inspired and filled by Spirit is divinely ordained to speak, no matter if male or female. Similarly, in the Gospel of Thomas (114) Jesus lays out his vision of the fully realized and perfected human being as one who both integrates and ultimately transcends all gender identification by becoming a "living spirit."

The most prominent of the noncanonical texts that feature Mary's leadership in conflict with Peter's jealousy is the Gospel of Mary. Whereas in the canonical Acts of the Apostles the leader figures are Peter and Paul, here it is Mary Magdalene who emerges as the preeminent disciple with the deepest understanding of the Master's teaching and the best ability to live life in accordance with this profound insight. Indeed, Mary steps in when the other disciples are in despair and intercedes with the Savior for them. The Gospel of Mary (17:10—19:5) relates the following episode. When the disciples, disheartened and terrified after the crucifixion, ask Mary Magdalene to comfort them by telling them the messages she has received in post—resurrection visions of Jesus, she agrees to confide to them the secret teachings. Andrew, however, rejects her teachings, and Peter questions her furiously: "Did he (Jesus), then, speak with a woman in private without our knowing about it? Are we to turn around and listen to her? Did he choose her over us?" Distressed at his rage, Mary weeps and replies: "My brother Peter...do you think that I have thought up these things by myself in my heart or that I am telling lies about the Savior?" Levi intervenes at this point to mediate the dispute: "Peter, you have always been hot—tempered...If the Savior made her (Mary) worthy, who are you to reject her? Surely the Savior's knowledge of her is completely reliable. That is why he loved her more than us."

Finally, the disciples agree to accept Mary's teachings. Encouraged by her words, they go out to preach. In examining these texts, it is clear that the two protagonists, Peter and Mary Magdalene, represent two distinctive approaches to the good news of the Christian story. While Peter grasps the fundamental tenets of the faith, holding them as historical facts, it is Mary who is in constant communion with the risen Christ, and is the recipient of ongoing revelation directly communicated from heart to heart, in silence. Yet in the end it was Peter who became the "rock" upon which the monolithic institutional Church emerged, modeled after the strictly hierarchical and patriarchal structures of the Roman Empire. Moreover, the "unbroken chain" between the apostle Peter (who later officially became the first "bishop of Rome") and the Pope served as the theological foundation for the "apostolic succession" that is the cornerstone of ministry and authority in the Church to this very day. The apostles had come to be seen *exclusively as male* – the evidence of the scriptures themselves notwithstanding.

Mary Magdalene's portrait in the noncanonical scriptures also strongly suggests that a connection exists between her and the Jewish wisdom tradition. In a text from first century Alexandria known as the Wisdom of Solomon, wisdom is portrayed as female and as the "spouse of the Lord" (this text was originally composed in Greek and refers to wisdom as Sophia – a synonym that is "feminine" from a grammatical or linguistic perspective). Wisdom/Sophia is a concept that is similar to the Jewish notion of the Shekinah, the feminine manifestation or presence of God's glory. As a quality, wisdom can of course be represented in either gender, yet ultimately it is deeply transpersonal. Divine wisdom is a transformational force to be actualized in all human beings, yet the virtues of wisdom are universally spurned. Bourgeault, among other scholars, argues that Mary Magdalene fully embodies the Sophia archetype. In Mary Magdalene, we witness the return and redemption of Sophia as the cherished partner and beloved of God. Bourgeault cautions us that this is *not* because Mary is a woman, but rather because she is a *transformed* woman, that is, a "living spirit," a fully realized and perfected human being.

This notion of unitive wisdom clearly transcends the dualistic mind with its insistence on paired (gender) opposites.

To conclude, the portrait of Mary Magdalene that emerges from these noncanonical texts is primarily based on three essential aspects that stand out in sharp contrast to the more familiar world of the canonical Gospels. First, Jesus' inner circle includes both men *and* women on an equal footing. Mary Magdalene is clearly in this inner circle. Second, Mary Magdalene is seen as "first among the apostles," not simply because she happens to be the first to witness the resurrection, but because she understands the true meaning of Jesus' teaching. Her position of leadership is earned and validated by Jesus himself. Third, she is clearly in a special relationship with Jesus. The nature of this relationship has for centuries been the subject of wild speculations and rumors, fueled by the recent craze generated by Dan Brown's *Da Vinci Code*. We will now more closely examine Mary's role as Jesus' "beloved disciple."

Mary Magdalene as Beloved

Dan Brown's *Da Vinci Code*, hypothesizes that Mary Magdalene and Jesus Christ were descendents of two houses of Israel (from King Saul and the tribe of Benjamin in the case of Mary; King David and the tribe of Judah in the case of Jesus), and that they were secretly married, forming a dynastic union between the houses. The anointing scene at Bethany was thus a ritual that a wife would perform over her soon—to—be—sacrificed husband and, at the same time, became a symbolic coronation, announcing Jesus as the Messiah, the "anointed one." The *Da Vinci Code* asserts that Mary Magdalene fled to France after the crucifixion, bearing a child who was Jesus' lineal descendent. The Holy Grail (*sainte grail*) that she carried was not the chalice from which Jesus drank at the Last Supper, but the royal bloodline (*sang real*) that flowed through their biological progeny. The child allegedly intermarried into the Frankish tribes, and the fruit of this union became a part of the Merovingian dynasty of French kings. Brown's hypothesis is based on the work of scholar Margaret Starbird and the so—called "bloodline conspiracy theory" of the British journalists Michael Baigent, Richard Leigh, and Henry Lincoln. The *Da Vinci Code* intrigued millions and infuriated nearly as many (mostly proponents of traditional Christianity) when the book was published in 2003.

The idea that Jesus Christ and Mary Magdalene were married draws inspiration from the Gospel of Philip, part of the Nag Hammadi collection. Both thematically and structurally, this gospel is geared toward nuptial union. The relationship between Mary Magdalene and Jesus is portrayed in terms that are openly erotic and spousal. Philip reports that Mary Magdalene walked continuously with Jesus, and that "the Savior loved her more than all the other disciples and kissed her often on her mouth" (Phil 63:33—64:9). Moreover, Mary is twice referred to as *koinonos*, a Greek term whose meanings can range from companion to consort, but which at any rate implies a committed partnership. Whatever the nature of this union, the Gospel of Philip lends itself to all sorts of projections and interpretations.

What are we to make of these assumptions? In the *Meaning of Mary Magdalene*, Cynthia Bourgeault argues that the *Da Vinci Code* hypothesis is not wrong, but that it's misdirected. In Bourgeault's words: "From the fruit of their love, Mary Magdalene and Jesus assuredly bore progeny, and they continue to do so. But this procreation is according to the ways of wisdom, not according to the ways of bloodline conspiracy."[25] What Mary Magdalene and Jesus were most prominently engaged in was a form of "spiritual begetting," a fully incarnate and "spiritually procreative" relationship that was deeply transformational. Their relationship was not contained within the boundaries of this world, but extended its intimacy beyond space and time.

Bourgeault, who draws deeply from the Christian contemplative tradition, suggests that Mary Magdalene and Jesus pursued a path that can best be characterized as "conscious love." This type of love is life affirming, inclusive, and implicitly relational in its nature; and it is absolutely and uncompromisingly self—giving. The term "conscious" makes clear that the touchstone is alchemical transformation, *not* simply romance. Bourgeault defines conscious love as love in the service of inner transformation.

Within the context of this love, the kisses Mary Magdalene receives on her mouth assume a different meaning. They are *not* a sign of sexual attraction or an illicit romance, but rather a sacred exchange, an expression of the interrelated ways and richly engendering spiritual love between Mary Magdalene and Jesus. In Near Eastern cultures, kissing on the mouth was practiced (and is still practiced today in some Sufi orders) as a transmission of spiritual knowledge and as a sacred exchange of being that implies the union of one breath with another. In all Semitic languages as well as in Greek and Latin, the word for "breath" is identical to the word for "spirit." To kiss and to breathe together is to partake of the same spirit. Two beings become one. Viewed in this context, the kissing on the mouth becomes a symbolic expression of a mystical union

---

[25] Bourgeault, *The Meaning of Mary Magdalene*, p. 192.

with one's "polar being" that takes place within the individual human heart. The act of kissing can hence be viewed as a foretaste of Mary Magdalene and Jesus' inner communion through which Spirit flows.

The path of conscious love can be lived and expressed in both celibate and noncelibate versions, according to Bourgeault. Yet chastity is, in either case, a requirement. She explains that chastity is not synonymous with celibacy, but that, instead, chastity is guarded by *purity of heart*. She leaves open the controversy over whether Mary Magdalene and Jesus engaged in sexual relations, and says that if they chose to give sexual expression to their union, "the pure embrace of their spiritual union would be reflected in the pure embrace of their human bodies."[26] In other words, Bourgeault expresses the view that the path of conscious love does not require sexual abstinence. Indeed, this path offers the option of engaging in sexual relations which, when purified from unwholesome attachments and egocentric cravings, are "truly eucharistic." This path of conscious love within the Christian esoteric tradition, which is comparable to the tantric traditions of the East, invites one, as Bourgeault says, "to give the innermost gift of oneself in the most intimate foretaste of divine union that can be known in human flesh."[27]

This approach makes the question of sexual relations between Mary Magdalene and Jesus secondary to the idea of conscious love. In addition, the making of Mary Magdalene into either "Jesus' sexual partner" or "his wife"–while acknowledging her inherent female sexuality–also carries within itself the problematic legacy

---

[26] Bourgeault, *The Meaning of Mary Magdalene*, p. 141.

[27] Bourgeault, p. 147.

of defining her exclusively through this reductionist and stereotypical lens. Feminist scholar Jane Schaberg cautions us *not* to confine Mary Magdalene to a romantic or personal relationship with Jesus, whether sexual or spiritual or both. To restrict Mary to a private relationship with Jesus carries the danger of perceiving her through the narrow lens of stereotypical "feminine" tasks of domestic service, mourning, caring for the dead, and playing a subordinate role to the male apostles who alone have a world—changing mission. In fact, Schaberg even argues that Mary should not be confined to *any* type of relationship with Jesus, but that we should try to see her in her own right. In Schaberg's words: "To resist the reduction and fragmentation of Mary Magdalene is to resist seeing her only as protagonist in a love or porno story, as madwoman, or victim, or lone hero, and also only as religious leader and intellectual. Attempting such resistance is resisting our own fragmentation."[28]

With that in mind, let us now consider an additional important function associated with Mary Magdalene. All four canonical Gospels report a highly dramatic incident at Bethany in which an unidentified woman (only in John is the woman identified specifically as Mary of Bethany) anoints Jesus' head and feet with precious perfume at a private dinner. Traditionally this woman is remembered to have been Mary Magdalene, which explains her numerous representations as the sorrowful woman holding an alabaster jar of anointing oil in Christian iconography and mythology. With the exception of Luke, the other three canonical Gospels set the incident directly before the crucifixion, and the episode takes on the meaning of a burial anointment. In Matthew and Mark,

---

[28] Schaberg, *The Resurrection of Mary Magdalene*, p. 352—353.

the unnamed woman anoints not the feet of Jesus but his head, which evokes the ceremonial act of anointing kings.

Jules Cashford and Anne Baring remind us that in ancient Sumer the ceremony of sacrificing the king and "son—lover" of the Goddess included an anointing ritual performed by the temple priestess. When viewed in this context, it is certainly an interesting coincidence that the name Magdalene literally signifies "she of the temple tower" or "watchtower." In *Mary Magdalene, Bride in Exile*, Margaret Starbird elaborates extensively on this anointing scene at Bethany. She argues that the scene amounts to a ritualistic proclamation of the kingship of Jesus in his role as the Messiah, which means the "anointed one," prior to his crucifixion. Starbird reminds us of the fact that the anointing act often carries explicit erotic associations in the poetry of the ancient Near East, as is apparent in the liturgical elements of the exquisite *Song of Songs* and other pre—Christian mythologies related to the ritualistic sacred marriage theme. Hence a thematic connection may exist between Mary Magdalene's anointing function at Bethany and *The Song of Songs*, which uses the fragrance of the oils of the Shulamite "sister—bride" as a metaphor for the ecstasy and sweetness of the intimate union between her and her bridegroom (4:10).

The Song of Songs later came to be interpreted by Jewish mystics as an allegory of the marriage covenant between God and the chosen people of Israel. Based on this extended metaphor, the Torah often equates idolatry with prostitution. The "idol—worshiping" Canaanite temple priestesses were perceived as a threat to the new Jewish religion. Well—versed in performing elaborate anointing rituals, the priestesses eventually came to be regarded as "temple prostitutes" engaged in ritualistic sex. This controversial characterization may also have contributed to the subsequent distorted notion of Mary Magdalene as "repentant prostitute."

While most modern scholars tend to take the Gospel of John at face value and, consequently, to perceive Mary of Bethany and Mary Magdalene as two distinctive female figures, Cynthia Bourgeault introduces a different perspective that is based on her long—term research and immersion in the contemplative Christian tradition. She concludes that John splits the Magdalenic personality into two parts, and that the traditional memory of Mary Magdalene as Jesus' anointer is substantially accurate. Valid reasons exist for keeping this part of her portrait intact, according to Bourgeault. One of the most compelling reasons is that Mary's anointing function holds the key to a deeper esoteric understanding of the Passion as an act of substituted love. Moreover, the anointing offers a powerful ritual to access the Christian pathway toward inner transformation and restoration to fullness of being. In other terms, by understanding this anointing ritual as an alchemical act of conscious love, in action far beyond what is commonly known as the sacrament of the "last unction" before death, both physical and spiritual wholeness can be restored. Bourgeault interprets the incident at Bethany, when Mary Magdalene ritually anoints Jesus' head and feet with precious oils, as the outer expression of the inner fragrance of their conscious love...characterized by the process of a continuous and mutual "inner anointing."

We do not know for certain what happened to Mary Magdalene after the resurrection. The Gospel bearing her name confirms that her spiritual leadership was honored in some circles of early Christianity. The "apostle to the apostles" may well have sojourned in France, where the fragrance of her sacred presence never completely disappeared from Christianity and lives on in French cultural memory, as shown by the popularity of her pilgrimage shrines in the basilicas at Baume and Vezelay. Indeed, in monastic love mysticism and allegory, in art and folklore, and in the love songs of the troubadours, her mysterious alchemical legacy was kept alive throughout the centuries.

From the Nethalloor Devi Temple

SHAKTISM: THE CELEBRATION OF MAHADEVI IN INDIA

Images of the Goddess are omnipresent in India and in contemporary Hinduism. The Goddess, or *Devi*, is alive and widely worshipped, especially in the Southern and Eastern part (the Bengal region) of India. Her effigy is painted on the sides of trucks, displayed on the walls of shops, and featured in private homes. Even Hindu devotees of male deities such as Krishna or Rama acknowledge the Divine Mother. In fact, the construction of a temple dedicated to a male deity must include at least one image of *Devi* to be considered consistent with Hindu thought.

The Goddess came to assume supreme significance in India during the tenth to the twelfth centuries CE, largely through the influence of the Tantra. The Tantra is an advanced system of yogic practices that includes manuals and "spiritual technologies" designed to expand the mystical awareness of spiritual practitioners. To uncover the undying divine reality at the core of their being, tantrics focus on visualization, contemplation, meditation, devotion, yoga, selfless service, study, and self—inquiry. Western authors often incorrectly equate the term "tantric" with stereotypical ideas about "yogic sexuality." Spiritualized sexuality is an important, but comparatively minor, part of the tantric tradition as a whole. Tantric practitioners aspire to maintain a meditative focus in order to make sacred even ordinary acts of life such as eating, breathing, working, and engaging in committed sexual relations. While classical yoga was commonly pursued by ascetics and renunciates attempting to escape from the vicissitudes of "worldly" life, tantric practices were often taken up by men and women who lived with their families in the marketplace and were committed to making their daily lives spiritually meaningful. The tantrics also maintained that liberation could be attained in this very lifetime by fulfilling one's social responsibilities and by actively engaging in *this* world.

The tantric Goddess tradition is referred to as Shaktism, and the devotees of *Devi* are called *shaktas*. The term *shakti* refers to the primordial energy or consciousness that gave birth to the cosmos out of its infinite essence while lovingly attending to the needs of all life – both human and other—than—human. *Shakti* is the divine power that transforms inanimate matter into life. In India, this dynamic cosmic life force is conceived of as feminine and is affilitated with the numerous manifestations of the Divine Mother. Unlike Western civilization, in which the goddesses are viewed as the mythological figures of pre—Christian cultures, *shaktas* conceive of *Devi* as the living matrix from which the universe and all of life springs.

Shaktism maintains that it is ultimately for the purpose of the evolution of human culture and consciousness that the Divine Mother created the manifest world. *Devi* worship involves both metaphysical principles and an anthropomorphic "personal" Goddess. In a medieval Hindu classic called *The Mystery of the Triune Goddess*, the Divine Mother proclaims: "Who and what I really am – cosmic awareness so vast I effortlessly hold trillions of universes in the palm of my hand – is beyond the capacity of human minds to understand. Therefore imagine me in whatever form appeals to you, and I promise in that very form I will come to you."[29] The Supreme Reality is *One*. It is referred to as *Nirguna Brahman*, one of the many names of the Divine in Hindu thought. *Nirguna Brahman* is the Transcendent Reality beyond form and all dualist notions of gender. Yet as form, or *Saguna Brahman*, the Supreme Consciousness may assume both male and female features.

Hinduism differs greatly from the Abrahamic religions in that it offers a rich and colorful set of Goddess iconography. Indeed, *Mahadevi* is a composite figure that features innumerable names and appears in a myriad of contrasting manifestations, each denoting different symbols, narratives, and aspects of the one Supreme Reality. In fact, the Divine Mother has so many attributes in India that it is common for her devotees to chant a set of thousand of her names as part of their spiritual practice. For example, *Mahadevi* is Uma, the moon—faced yogini of the Himalayas, the white—skinned Gauri of the *Brahmins* (the priestly caste), and the dark—skinned Kalika of the tantrics.

---

[29] Johnsen, *The Living Goddess*, p. 4—5.

She is Chandika in Calcutta and Bhavani in Maharashtra.
In Brindaban, where Krishna lived, she is his beloved
Radha. *Devi* is worshiped in all of her life cycles: At one
year of age, she is known under the name of Sandhya.
And, at the age of sixteen, she is venerated as Lalita.
Interestingly, at her shrine in Vindhyachal near the sacred
city of Benares at the Ganges, *Devi* has been worshiped
for centuries as the bird—headed goddess Vindhya
Vasini. This may reveal an unbroken continuity of her
veneration since the Neolithic period. Archaeological
evidence indicates that the worship of the Goddess in
India originated during the ancient Indus River Valley
civilization dating to the second and third millennia BCE,
or even earlier.

Yet it is in the mythic narratives known as the Puranas
(300—900 CE), many centuries later, that the Divine
Feminine finds its greatest expression in Hindu literature.
Major Shakta texts such as the *Devi Bhagavatam Purana* and
the *Lalita Mahatmyam* recount the story of the Goddess.
Mahadevi is worshipped in two basic and contrasting
modes: the gentle, nurturing, benevolent manifestations
on the one hand; and the terrifying, destructive, and fierce
manifestations on the other. This is a reflection of the
notion that the Divine Feminine is both: the source *and* the
dissolution of all life.

In her benevolent appearances, *Devi* is viewed as an icon
of fertility, maternal abundance, and marital loyalty–
especially in her function as the consort of male Hindu
deities. As the popular and gentle goddess Lakshmi,
Devi is affiliated with the god Vishnu and his two most
prominent incarnations: Krishna and Rama. In Hindu
iconography, Lakshmi is commonly depicted as a beautiful
woman in a red sari, seated or standing on a pink lotus,
symbol of purity and immortality. She is flanked by

auspicious white elephants and pours gold coins from the palm of one of her hands. Lakshmi represents abundance, beauty, and good health. She grants a happy and harmonious family life. Not surprisingly, the Hindu bride is commonly viewed as an embodiment of this goddess. As Sarasvati, *Devi* is the consort of the god Brahma. Sarasvati, the much beloved "Hindu Muse," inspires all forms of creative and artistic expression. Her lute is viewed as a symbol of the primordial sound vibrations of the universe. As the goddess of wisdom, speech, and knowledge, Sarasvati is also known as the "Mother of the Vedas," the sacred books of Hinduism recorded in Sanskrit. *Devi* tends to be more subordinate in her role as a consort.

In her terrifying and fierce manifestations as Kali or Durga, the Goddess takes on a much more autonomous role, emerging as the great protectress of the cosmic order and as the fearless warrioress with the power to destroy all illusions. *Devi's* more autonomous appearances may serve as an empowering role model for women across cultures.

Kali – The Dark—Skinned Mother Adorned with Skulls

O Kali, my Mother full of bliss!
Enchantress of the almighty Shiva!
In Thy delirious joy Thou dancest,
Clapping Thy hands together!
Thou art the Mover of all that move,
And we are but Thy helpless toys..."
— *Ramakrishna Paramhansa*

The esoteric—mystical interpretation of the goddess Kali in tantric Hinduism is complex and multi—layered. In her terrifying manifestation, Kali, the "Dark One," appears at first glance gruesome and repellent to most Westerners. Although depictions of her as a maternal goddess exist, Kali is more often represented as an old woman with an emaciated body. Naked or half—naked, she appears with pendulous breasts, disheveled hair, sunken eyes, and a lolling tongue hanging from her bloodstained mouth. A garland of human skulls adorns her neck, and she displays a girdle of severed human arms and hands around her waist. The dark—skinned goddess is commonly represented as standing on a corpse or dancing her frenzied, uncontrollable dance in the midst of the burning pyres on the cremation grounds, surrounded by jackals, snakes, and ghosts. Kali's multiple arms variously hold a bloody sword, a noose, a freshly severed head, and a skull cup filled with blood. What are we to make of this horrifying representation?

Kali's terrifying appearance invites all sorts of misconceptions. To get an accurate understanding of her multilayered esoteric significance we need to go beyond her physical appearance. Kali's nakedness symbolizes her knowledge of the "naked" or perfect Truth beyond the veils of delusion. The human skulls and the girdle represent finite worldly attachments that are being destroyed by the "Dark Mother," if we invoke her. As an embodiment of divine knowledge and wisdom, Kali shatters all illusions. She is the force that governs and stops time. Everything originates from her and, ultimately, is devoured by her at the moment of death. The blood sacrifices performed in her honor at her temple in Calcutta, the *Kalighat*, have ancient roots. They were already an integral part of religious rites during the Vedic Age, which dates back to the second millennium BCE, and they may have survived in the tradition of Indian village cults aimed at propitiating evil spirits viewed as harbingers of disease and natural calamities. These sacrifices commonly include various kinds of animals equated with human desires and attachments, all of which must be sacrificed to Kali before liberation may be attained. As the mistress of sacrificial blood symbolizing the life force, Kali presides over the mysteries of life and death. As the life—giver, the blood of her creation has to be offered back to her. Yet in this context we may note that animal offerings are generally on the wane in contemporary Shaktism. Also, Brahmins who perform these sacrifices are instructed to avoid causing the animals unnecessary pain and suffering.

During the *puja* (worshiping ritual), the sacrificial blood is used as an offering to the consecrated icon of Kali and to bless her devotees. The sacrificial flesh is cooked and served to the poor and disenfranchised, provided they have a nonvegetarian diet. Some *shaktas* will substitute animals with pumpkin offerings, or red flowers may be used to symbolize the blood offerings. Sacrificial offerings are primarily an exoteric or "external" expression of religion. Yet when viewed from a deeper esoteric perspective, the "animal" that needs to be "sacrificed" is our ego—centered self, which creates dualistic notions and keeps us in a state of separateness and alienation from the divine and ourselves. Moreover, every living being is ultimately destined to become a sacrifice on the "altar of time." Kali's necklace of severed skulls hence also symbolizes the dissolution of the world of forms and objects back into the Goddess herself, where the apparent duality of matter and spirit is transcended. With her lolling tongue Kali drinks the intoxicating "blood—wine" of ignorance, assisting her devotees to quench their thirst and unconscious desire for endless rebirths. From an esoteric perspective, Kali's terrifying appearance may be viewed symbolically as a positive expression of her power to shatter illusions.

The fifty skulls comprising Kali's garland are said to
represent the fifty letters of the sacred Sanskrit alphabet.
Like other religious traditions, Hinduism tells us that
the "word" or "sound" emanated from Brahman, the
Supreme Consciousness. Eventually, this divine speech or
sound generated primordial matter (for a more detailed
account of Hindu Cosmology and Creation Mythology
see the e—book *In the Beginning: Creation Narratives
Across Cultures* in the *One Truth, Many Paths* series). In
Hindu thought, the Goddess is commonly identified
with *prakriti*, the material world. Kali is worshiped as
the great protectress who guards us from the harm
caused by natural calamities such as floods, droughts,
fires, earthquakes, famines, and diseases. Kali's frenzied
dance on the cremation grounds is an expression of
the primordial vibrations of the universe, the creative
divine impulse that transforms inanimate matter into
life. Creation continues as long as the universe exists
because the creative process is ultimately an expression
of God's love for life in all its facets. In the end, life itself
with its continuous evolution is the dance. Kali's dance
is this ever—unfolding cycle of life and death. As the
creative divine impulse, the Goddess is the force that rules
evolution as apparent in the cycles of nature and time:
eons, ages, seasons, day and night.

Kali also personifies the dark moon – as does her Greek
counterpart Hecate, Goddess of the Crossroads and
"Queen of the Night." In premodern lunar symbolism
across the cultures, the three days of the dark moon
represented a period of gestation before the reappearance
of the crescent heralding another cycle of light and life.
Interestingly though, darkness and death were *not* viewed
as antagonistic to light and life but rather as another
essential aspect of the Goddess. Similarly, the "Dark
Mother" across all cultures and religions represents the

dissolution of the cosmos, for all colors disappear in black just as the manifest world dissolves back into her. Kali's blackness may also be viewed as symbolizing the darkest and most fertile layers in the womb of the earth. Plants wither and die, subsequently serving as nutrients for new growth in the depths. Life and death are intertwined. Kali's dance, although threatening complete destruction, contains within its essence the seeds for a new cycle of creation. As the activating principle, Kali paradoxically embodies both functions: the great deluder and devouring Mother on the one hand, and the life—giving and benevolent Mother on the other. In her two primary modes, the entire universe becomes Kali's playground, her *lila* or "divine play." The "Dark Mother" helps us release everything that blocks our psycho—spiritual evolution, purifying us in the searing fire of loss and suffering. She leads us through the harrowing encounter with death and dissolution to the psycho—spiritual wholeness and profound freedom that lies within. In confronting and assimilating death in its most concrete form, Kali assists us in overcoming our fear of death.

Through her *maya*, her beguiling powers, Kali plays the grand cosmic game of life and death that ensnares us in the web of worldly desires only to destroy our fears and finite attachments, hereby revealing the Supreme Truth.

Shiva and Shakti: The Archetypal Union of the Feminine and Masculine

In another popular representation, Kali stands on the corpselike body of her consort, the god Shiva. As she tramples on his prostrate body, her energy revives him. Kali's uninhibited stance is strikingly demonstrated in those scenes where she sits on top of Shiva's motionless body. When impregnated by Shiva, Kali assumes the role of the cosmic Mother who brings forth the entire universe from her creative womb. In this context, the Goddess embodies the dynamic and ever—unfolding life force of creation. She *is* Shiva's *Shakti*. Shiva himself is viewed as pure and ineffable consciousness without beginning and end. Shiva does not act in the world. He is the Unmanifest. A popular saying in India maintains that Shiva would be a corpse without Shakti.

In Hindu life cycle rituals such as puberty and marriage, the presence of the Goddess is invoked and the woman herself is viewed as an embodiment of Shakti.

Depictions of Kali on Shiva's motionless body stand in sharp contrast to representations of the Sacred Feminine in other religious traditions, which view the feminine archetype as subordinate and passive. Tantric Hinduism emphasizes the ultimate unity of the Supreme Reality beyond the multiplicity of the manifest world. Yet this nondual Reality expresses itself in two primary principles as the evolutionary process unfolds. These binary principles are variously called *purusha* (spirit) and *prakriti* (matter), or consciousness and shakti. The union of Shiva and Shakti, the embrace of God and Goddess, thus represents the nondual nature of the Supreme Truth. Similar to the concepts of *yin* and *yang* in Chinese Taoism, they are interdependent and cannot exist without the other – each contains the other within its essence. Shiva and Shakti are a divine whole that finds its expression in the apparent polarity of the "masculine" and the "feminine." Rather than viewing this polarity as interdependent and complementary, the human mind has a tendency to perceive the "masculine" and "feminine" as rigid and incompatible polar opposites; and more often than not these opposites are associated with stereotypical gender notions within a given socio—cultural context.

Tantrics emphasize the importance of piercing the veils of delusion that obscure the nondual essence of the Supreme Reality. Only if the energies of Shiva and Shakti are balanced and psycho—spiritually integrated *within* each one of us...will we be able to engage in sacred mystical union with our intimate partner.

From the perspective of tantric thought Kali is *not* the "terrifying Mother," for in the end nothing is destroyed. The world manifests, dissolves, and, eventually, reemerges in an ever—evolving cosmic display of life and death. The "Dark Mother" is horrifying to the ignorant, as she threatens to destroy the finite to reveal the Infinite; but to the wise she is an embodiment of the death of death, and her darkness reflects the dazzling brilliance of spiritual illumination. These functions of Kali are particularly underscored by two of her highly symbolic *mudras* (hand gestures). One of her hands invites her devotees to release all fears, while the other grants protection and infinite blessings. To her closest followers Kali is not only *prakriti*, the material world – she is also form and spirit, shakti and consciousness.

One of Kali's most ardent devotees was the great nineteenth—century Bengali saint Sri Ramakrishna, who served as her priest at the Dakshineshvar Temple in Calcutta. After experiencing his first vision of Kali at the age of twenty, he was absorbed in loving contemplation of her. He experienced the icon of the goddess as alive, and saw her leap down from the altar to dance ecstatically on the temple grounds. Perhaps the most striking feature in Ramakrishna's worship of Kali was his intimacy with her. He would ascend the altar to caress the Goddess, joking and laughing with her, and he offered rice curry to her while imploring her to eat. In every waking moment, Ramakrishna worshiped Kali as the all—knowing and all—merciful Mother of the Universe. To this day, her worship remains enormously popular in India.

Kali may serve as an empowering role model for Western women because of her largely autonomous function. In *Shakti Woman*, feminist writer Vicki Noble calls the Hindu goddess "an icon of liberated energy, spiritual freedom and the untamed spiritual nature. She is the Feminine in a much larger sense than any archetypes carried by Western culture for at least the last two thousand years..."[30] From a cross—cultural perspective, the archetypal image of the Gorgon—Medusa in classical Greek mythology may come closest to Kali's iconography and symbolism. Similar to Kali, Medusa is depicted with protruding tongue, bulging eyes, and snakes in her hair. One gaze from her eyes can turn men to stone. Yet in some of her representations she assumes a classic birthing posture, squatting (this may point to her earlier function as a birthing goddess.) As the archetypal "Terrible Mother" of classical Greece, the Medusa was largely demonized by patriarchal Western culture, although she clearly possesses regenerative and sexual powers according to Noble.

---

[30] Noble, *Shakti Woman*, p. 200.

CONCLUSION

The Divine Feminine expresses itself in an incredibly rich and multi—faceted array of manifestations, names, symbols, and archetypal qualities, and is an essential part of our cultural legacy that is too often ignored or dismissed in studies on comparative religion. Like other spiritual paths, the path of the Goddess may serve as a gateway to transformation and conscious evolution. Yet this outcome depends on *how we relate to the Divine Feminine*. As author, activist, and Jungian analyst Jean Shinoda Bolen points out, if we are unaware of our intrinsic capacity for autonomy, courage, strength, and sensuality as women, archetypal role models such as the goddesses Inanna, Kali, Athena, Isis, or Oshun can remind us to get in touch with these qualities within our psyches. By visualizing particular manifestations of the Divine Feminine, and by reading the mythic narratives as related to these goddesses, we may be able to access the deeper archetypal patterns within us and, eventually, we will be able to express our unique gifts and talents in a more empowered way.

We also need to be aware that potential pitfalls exist in relation to the concept of the Divine Feminine. First, if we identify ourselves exclusively with the exoteric dimension of Goddess worship, without doing the deep and often painful inner work, we may conclude that we are Goddess embodiments in our own right and therefore, by definition, "superior" to anybody else. This viewpoint reflects the hierarchical structures of superiority that have, for thousands of years, characterized patriarchal institutions and paradigms of the major religious systems. Second, we may also be tempted to use arbitrary and highly problematic judgments about so—called "masculine" and "feminine" qualities attributed to specific concepts of the divine that are all too often the product of socio—cultural and personal conditioning. We need to remember that Spirit, in its very essence, is transpersonal – that is, it transcends gender polarities and all anthropomorphic expressions and conceptions of the divine. Finally, the question remains: What, exactly, do we mean when we talk about the Divine Feminine, or, more specifically, the Goddess?

The term "Goddess" doesn't have to refer to an omnipotent, omniscient supreme "Mother in Heaven" – a counterpart to the anthropomorphic concept of "God the Father" that is still so widespread in traditional mainstream Christianity. Both these anthropomorphic notions of the divine reflect what Ken Wilber repeatedly refers to as the "mythic God or Goddess," that is, one particular aspect of the second Face of God or Goddess as the "Great Thou" that is relational. Wilber argues that the notion of the mythic God or Goddess represents a major impediment to transpersonal conscious evolution because it originates in the premodern period at a time when humans lacked the capacity to conceptualize and think in terms of higher abstraction. For example, numerous images of the great Goddess date back to the Neolithic period, which was predominantly horticultural (the term 'horticulture' refers to a farming culture that is based on a hoe or simple digging stick easily used by women as opposed to the heavy animal—drawn iron plow of later agrarian societies). Because these images originated in the premodern or prerational period, they are not necessarily helpful role models for modern and postmodern humans, according to Wilber. Moreover, many of these anthropomorphic notions of the divine are based on limited and limiting human projections that are problematic insofar as they come with a persistent and complex legacy of socio—cultural and personal conditioning.

Problems arise if we perceive the Goddess exclusively through the lens of a horticultural planting mythology and become overly identified or attached to one particular notion of the Divine Feminine. The Divine Feminine, like the Divine Masculine, ultimately transcends all stages of consciousness and culture as well as all preconceived notions and stereotypical concepts. Modern and postmodern humans can take the primary distinction between the descending and the ascending paths of Spirit into consideration. In *A Brief History of Everything*, Ken Wilber describes these two primary modes of Spirit as follows:

> *"The Feminine Face of Spirit – the Goddess – is preeminently Agape, or Compassion, the descending and immanent and manifesting current of the Kosmos, the principle of embodiment, and bodily incarnation, and relationship, and relational and manifest embrace, touching each and every being with perfect and equal grace, rejecting nothing, embracing all...Whereas the Masculine Face of Spirit – or God – is preeminently the ascending and transcendental current of the Kosmos that strives to find greater wholeness...and rises to unending revelations of a greater Good and Glory by breaking the limits and reaching for the sky...the Feminine Face of Spirit embraces the Many with Goodness and immanent care...She is the overall movement of Efflux, the entire movement of creative Descent and Superabundance at each and every epoch...The cure is no longer regression to horticultural mythology, but*

progression to Goddess embodiment in the forms of today's integrations [emphasis added by author]."[31]

This is the great paradox of Spirit, which is both fully immanent and transcendent. As the descending mode of Spirit manifests in the world of form, the Divine Feminine is all—encompassing in the sense that it embraces the paradoxes inherent in the human condition. Wilber opines that this includes all historical epochs and all stages of consciousness and culture, including patriarchy. Consequently, Wilber argues that the Goddess cannot be reduced to a mythological figure pertaining to premodern horticultural societies, nor could she possibly ever have been obliterated by any of the patriarchal institutions and paradigms. The Goddess was never really "dead." What cannot be denied, however, is the collective psychological repression of the "Great Mother" archetype that gradually occurred over time in most of the world's cultures. The hiding place of the Goddess archetype was, indeed, the collective unconscious.

Now, as humanity finds itself in this major transition, conceptions of the Goddess can re—emerge. As the entire "energetic efflux of creative descent," to use Wilber's term, the Goddess is the divine matrix out of which all forms of the manifest world arise in each and every epoch. She is the container holding all paradoxes. The Goddess imparts vital energy, she is the life force that represents and evokes the inherent creative potential in all beings. This is the intriguing evolutionary perspective of Barbara Marx Hubbard, renowned social innovator, author, visionary, and leader of the new worldview of conscious evolution.

---

[31] Wilber, *A Brief History of Everything*, p. 232. See also *Sex, Ecology, Spirituality*, p. 692—93.

Marx Hubbard focuses on the accelerated rise and emergence of the evolutionary woman, whom she calls the "Feminine Co—Creator."

She explains that for the first time in thousands of years, women now have the opportunity to give birth to their authentic feminine "Self," and to actively participate in the workings of the evolutionary process. Marx Hubbard refers to the modern and postmodern rise of women into the role of evolutionary agents as an event of the highest significance. She emphasizes that the Feminine Co—Creator is *not* seeking to be equal to men by emulating them, which would only reinforce and perpetuate some of the existing dysfunctional patterns. Rather, this new evolutionary woman is engaged in a partnership with evolutionary men, fully participating in the process of conscious co—creation as opposed to the more dualistic and confrontational approach of postmodernist feminism. According to Marx Hubbard, the balance of the feminine with the masculine is, in fact, vital for the emergence of a new evolutionary synthesis.

At the time of this writing, the new archetype of the Feminine Co—Creator is still in its infancy within modern and postmodern Western culture. But if women are willing to embrace the totality of their psycho—spiritual power and intellectual potential; and to integrate their shadow selves, spiritual immanence, and the bond of communion with all life forms, they will likely make vital contributions to the evolutionary process.

At this critical juncture in time and history, the Goddess may well express herself through this new archetype of the Feminine Co—Creator, who chooses to consciously engage in the process of evolution as we face major global challenges and witness the emergence of new paradigms and values. Evolution is continuously unfolding, and the intrinsic urge toward creation and innovation in both men and women is an ideal expression of Spirit's passionate love for life.

ACKNOWLEDGMENTS

Words are sometimes not enough to express our gratitude. This book would not have been possible without the unwavering support of the following individuals: my editor Sari Friedman who believed in me and worked tirelessly, providing her invaluable input and insights. Brenda Knight, champion of my book and my liaison to the publisher, who provided her seasoned advice and steady guidance throughout the long journey toward publication. The team at Mango who designed the beautiful book cover and assisted me with all technical aspects related to book production. I would also like to thank all my friends for their continuous support and encouragement along the way. And last but not least, I would like to express my gratitude to my beloved husband Rod Price for his patience and steady support, which kept me going through all the vicissitudes that were inevitably part of this journey.

BIBLIOGRAPHY

Badejo, Diedre. *Osun Seegesi: The Elegant Deity of Wealth, Power and Femininity*. Trenton, New Jersey: Africa World Press Inc., 1996.

Baring Anne and Jules Cashford. *The Myth of the Goddess: Evolution of an Image*. New York: Arkana (Penguin Books), 1991.

Barstow, Anne. *The Prehistoric Goddess*. In *The Book of the Goddess*, edited by Carl Olson, p.7—15. New York: Crossroad Publishing, 1983.

Begg, Ean. *The Cult of the Black Virgin*. London: Arkana (Routledge & Kegan Paul), 1985.

Birnbaum Chiavola, Lucia. *Dark Mother: African Origins and Godmothers*. San Jose, CA: iUniverse Inc., 2001.

Bolen Shinoda, Jean. *Goddesses in Everywoman: Powerful Archetypes for Women*. Harper&Row, 1984.

_____. *Urgent Message from Mother*. Boston, MA: Conari Press, 2005.

Bonder, Saniel. *Healing the Spirit/Matter Split*. Mt. Tam Empowerments Inc., Edition 2008.

Bourgeault, Cynthia. *The Meaning of Mary Magdalene*. Boston & London: Shambhala, 2010.

Brown, Mackenzie C. *Kali, the Mad Mother*. In *The Book of the Goddess*, edited by Carl Olson, p.110—123. New York: Crossroad Publishing, 1983.

Canan, Janine (ed). *Messages from Amma: In the Language of the Heart*. Berkeley, CA: Celestial Arts, 2004.

Christ, Carol. *Rebirth of the Goddess: Finding Meaning in Feminist Spirituality*. New York: Routledge, 1997.

Crowley, Vivianne. *Wicca: A Comprehensive Guide to the Old Religion in the Modern World*. London: Element (HarperCollins), 2003.

Daniel, Yvonne. *Dancing Wisdom: Embodied Knowledge in Haitian Vodou, Cuban Yoruba, and Bahian Candomble*. Urbana & Chicago: University of Illinois Press, 2005.

Eisler, Riane. *The Chalice and the Blade*. HarperSanFrancisco, 1995.

Gadon, Elinor. *The Once and Future Goddess: A Sweeping Visual Chronicle of the Sacred Female and Her Reemergence in the Cultural Mythology of Our Time*. HarperSanFrancisco, 1989.

Gilligan, Carol. *In a Different Voice: Psychological Theory and Women's Development*. Harvard University Press, 1982.

Gimbutas, Marija. *The Living Goddesses*. Berkeley: University of California Press, 1999.

Harvey, Andrew. *The Essential Mystics*. New Jersey: Castle Books, 1998.

Houston, Jean. *The Passion of Isis and Osiris*. New York: Ballantine/Wellspring, 1995.

Jagannathan, Shakunthala. *Hinduism: An Introduction*. Mumbai, India: Vakils, Feffer and Simons Ltd., 1984.

Johnsen, Linda. *The Living Goddess: Reclaiming the Tradition of the Mother of the Universe*. St. Paul, MN: YES International Publishers, 1999.

Judith, Anodea. *Waking the Global Heart*, Santa Rosa, CA: Elite Books, 2006.

King, Karen. *The Gospel of Mary of Magdala*. Santa Rosa, CA: Polebridge Press, 2003.

Klostermaier, Klaus. *Hinduism: A Short History*. Oxford: Oneworld Publications, 2000.

Knapp, Bettina. *Isis: Harmony of Flesh/Spirit/Logos*. In *Women in Myth*, p.1—20. State University of New York Press, 1997.

Marx Hubbard, Barbara. *Birth 2012 and Beyond: Humanity's Great Shift to the Age of Conscious Evolution*. Shift Books, 2012.

Monaghan, Patricia. *The Goddess Companion*. St. Paul, MN: Llewellyn Publications, 1999.

Murphy, Joseph. *Oshun the Dancer*. In *The Book of the Goddess*, edited by Carl Olson, p. 190—201. New York: Crossroad Publishing, 1983.

Neumann, Erich. *The Great Mother: An Analysis of the Archetype*. New Jersey: Princeton University Press, 1974.

Nicholson, Sarah. *The Evolutionary Journey of Woman: From the Goddess to Integral Feminism*. Tucson, AZ: Integral Publishers, 2013.

Noble, Vicki. *Shakti Woman: Feeling our Fire, Healing our World*. HarperSanFrancisco, 1991.

Ochshorn, Judith. *Ishtar and Her Cult*. In *The Book of the Goddess*, edited by Carl Olson, p.16—27. New York: Crossroad Publishing, 1983.

Purce, Jill. *The Mystic Spiral*. New York: Thames & Hudson Inc., 2003.

Radford Ruether, Rosemary. *Goddesses and the Divine Feminine*. Berkeley: University of California Press, 2005.

Rigoglioso, Marguerite. *The Cult of the Divine Births in Ancient Greece*. New York: Palgrave Macmillan, 2009.

_____. *Virgin Mother Goddesses of Antiquity*. New York: Palgrave Macmillan, 2010.

Schaberg, Jane. *The Resurrection of Mary Magdalene*. New York: The Continuum International Publishing Group Inc., 2002.

Shlain, Leonard. *The Alphabet versus the Goddess: The Conflict between Word and Image*. Viking Penguin, 1998.

Starbird, Margaret. *Mary Magdalene: Bride in Exile*. Rochester, Vermont: Bear & Company, 2005.

Starhawk. *The Spiral Dance: A Rebirth of the Ancient Religion of the Great Goddess*. HarperSanFrancisco, 1999.

Stone, Merlin. *When God was a Woman*. New York: Barnes & Noble Books, 1993.

Teish, Luisah. *Jambalaya*. New York: HaperOne, 1985.

Warner, Marina. *Alone of Her Sex: The Myth and Cult of the Virgin Mary*. London: Pan Books (Picador), 1985.

Wilber, Ken. *A Brief History of Everything*. Boston: Shambhala, 2000.

_____. *Sex, Ecology, Spirituality*. Boston: Shambhala, 2000.

Willetts, R.F., *Cretan Cults and Festivals*. London: Routledge & Kegan Paul, 1962.

Woodman, Marion, and Elinor Dickson. *Dancing in the Flames: The Dark Goddess in the Transformation of Consciousness*. Boston, MA: Shambhala, 1996.

Woodman, Marion, and Robert Bly. *The Maiden King: The Reunion of the Masculine and Feminine*. New York: Henry Holt & Co., 1998.

AUTHOR BIO

Isabella Price, MA, is an international speaker, author, and higher education professional at JFK University where she teaches "World Spirituality" courses. Isabella is the author of the leading-edge book series "One Truth, Many Paths" on the world's wisdom traditions, which includes her book *Goddess Power* on the Sacred Feminine. For over twenty-five years, she has been successfully teaching classes and workshops at JFK University, the California College of the Arts, and numerous other educational institutions and religious venues. She has traveled extensively and participated in numerous rituals from diverse wisdom traditions. She holds an MA in the humanities (global history and comparative religion) from the University of Zurich, Switzerland. She is also a certified SQ21 Spiritual Intelligence coach and teaches meditation to veterans suffering from PTSD and other community members. She lives in the San Francisco Bay Area with her husband and two felines.

CPSIA information can be obtained
at www.ICGtesting.com
Printed in the USA
BVOW09s1448240917
495654BV00001B/1/P